WHAT PEOPLE ARE SAYING ABOUT

PAGAN PORTALS – YOUR FAERY MAGIC

There are some who say that the realms of Faery lie just beneath our own; they are the realms of ever-becoming, as the forces of nature that govern the green and growing world. *Your Faery Magic* invites you to open to the deep soul of nature with a delightful collection of imaginative and playful rituals. Open your Faery Heart and rekindle a sense of enchantment in your life!

Sharon Knight

This is a warm and innovative book, ideal for someone experiencing the first inklings of a need for re-enchantment. Gentle souls seeking inspiration may find this is a good path to explore.

Nimue Brown

T0154606

Pagan Portals
Your Faery Magic

Discover what it means to be fey and
unlock your natural power

Pagan Portals
Your Faery Magic

Discover what it means to be fey and
unlock your natural power

Halo Quin

Winchester, UK
Washington, USA

First published by Moon Books, 2015
Moon Books is an imprint of John Hunt Publishing Ltd., Laurel House, Station Approach,
Alresford, Hants, SO24 9JH, UK
office1@jhpbooks.net
www.johnhuntpublishing.com
www.moon-books.net

For distributor details and how to order please visit the 'Ordering' section on our website.

Text copyright: Halo Quin 2015

ISBN: 978 1 78535 076 4
Library of Congress Control Number: 2015943099

A CIP catalogue record for this book is available from the British Library.

Design: Lee Nash

Printed and bound by CPI Group (UK) Ltd, Croydon, CR0 4YY, UK

We operate a distinctive and ethical publishing philosophy in all
areas of our business, from our global network of authors to
production and worldwide distribution.

CONTENTS

I dedicate this book to my Mother, who taught me to love the green world and respect it as alive and aware, and to the Queen of Faery and her people, who guide me on this path each and every day.

Gratitude

This book exists because of so many people, from my mother who taught me to love trees to the teachers at school who never once told me Faeries weren't real (and in fact encouraged me to dream the opposite...) but there are more recent, more obvious hands involved, which I feel deserve explicit acknowledgement. Firstly, the Spanish Reclaiming community, Morgaine, Samuel and Morri in particular, who brought me firmly back home to Faeryland and encouraged me to do this work when I needed the push the most. T. Thorn Coyle who taught me that power begins at home. Erin Kavanagh who encouraged me to dust the text off and give it another go. The original sponsors of *The Faery Heart*, my first book and the foundation of this one: Gwydion Blackrose, Ian Cookesley, Cassandra, Marie Geever, Margit Ströbele, Fortuna, Niki Whiting, Shira, Paul Rousselle, Marion McCartney, Amanda Strong and Alison Wood. Claudia Lohman deserves a very special mention as the person who really helped me make this book what it is now, tirelessly editing and re-editing those raw words into something that belongs in a bookshop. And my sweetheart, James, who has stood by me through excitements and disappointments, forging ahead and giving up...on this as with every other adventure.

Thank you to all the Witches and Faeries and fey folk who have supported me in my work. I hope I've done you all proud!

The Invitation

I invite you now to join me on a journey into the heart of the world.

This is a space to play, to discover our own hearts and to discover the heart of Faery.

Here you will find stories and musings about the fae, Faeryland and our hearts as humans.

I'm not going to pretend that I believe the fae to be all fluffy and light, but I will tell you that I believe they, as beings or as a concept, hold a key to unlocking the place we hold deep within ourselves, where our true desires, our magic, lives.

This is not a book for spectators; it is for people who long to travel down this path, who long to unlock their hearts and the wonder of Faery.

This is my path of the heart, of beauty and play and of coming alive, and it can be your path if you choose.

Join me, walk with me, dance with me!

The way is long and the weather is changeable, but if you can keep hold of that desire to know yourself, if you make a commitment to honesty and integrity and choose to seek, like the young adventurers in those Faery tales you may once have heard, with a willingness to learn and share and be delighted, then your courage shall be rewarded. However hard the path, there are treasures waiting for you in the Faery Heart of yourself.

Will you join me? Yes?

Then come, hear the music, follow the path.

The path of the Faery Heart.

Chapter 1

In the Beginning...

A Creation Story

Long before time was time, the Earth was born of stardust. She lived and breathed. Her heart beat. Her soul sang into the universe, singing in chorus with her brothers and sisters, the other planets. The stars, older than she and her siblings, watched and loved her, knowing the young planets to be kin.

The heart of the Earth beat. Each beat held a spirit and each spirit danced between the centre of the Earth and the realm of the stars. The stars, too, had hearts which beat, their heartbeats each held a spirit and these spirits danced with the heartbeats of the Earth and all were together. These beings, which arose from the heart of the Earth and the stars, were the fey ones.

The Earth began to grow. As she settled into her skin she drew the sky around her like a cloak and in the warmth between the sky and her skin, the plants grew and oceans settled. From the wombs of her oceans, animals were born, animals which grew and changed. Some grew into feathered beings, some into reptiles, some into furred ones and some, eventually, into humans.

The fae were fascinated by the beings birthed from the Earth and they watched carefully as we grew and developed. They guided us, played with us, danced with us through our early years. And we danced with the fae and all the other beings of the land and sky and sea.

But over time we humans found great power and in our rush to be great, we began to lose sight of the heart of our Mother Earth. We stopped hearing the songs of the stars. For us, their hearts had stopped beating. And when we stopped hearing the heartbeat of our mother, we stopped seeing how she was alive. It became easier for us to use her without giving back, without remembering that we are a part of her. Our power over the land grew great and in the flush of amazement, we were lost in the maze that led away from gentle wonders, we lost sight of our relationships with the other beings of this world. We went from weak to strong, but we forgot where the spirit that fed our strength lived… We forgot that there is strength in wonder and vulnerability and we donned our armour of brittle power, forgetting the ones who had opened our eyes to the possibility of possibility.

And so the spirits of the heart of the stars and the Earth became sad. The bright ones, the dark ones, the dancing ones, they drifted back into the heart of the Earth, to roam upon the upper lands only in times of celebration or sorrow, to remind us of our kin. The distance proved so great we forgot how to see them, we forgot to listen to the heartbeat of the Faery realms.

The worlds drifted apart. We lived in one world, where all is matter, which we believe is for us to use. They lived in another, where all things are alive and related to each other. And they wept, and we grew in power while we also, bit by bit, forgot the essence of joy.

But do not despair, for there is more to the tale than this great divide between spirit and matter, magic and material; for every night and day that the Faery host roamed, there would be one who told the tale. For every moment when the worlds became close again, kissing, one with eyes to see and ears to hear might find themselves dancing to the music of the fae, the enchantment of the heartbeat of the Earth. And every time the fae from the stars descended, we were reminded of the glorious beauty of life beyond the dust of the world we had chosen to walk within. These moments were passed on as stories, stories shared over campfires, at bedtime, in songs by those with Faery Hearts, hearts that still hear the song of the Earth's heartbeat.

The stories begin to weave a web, a picture. Some stories tell of those fae beings who cause trouble, some of those who help, some of great beauty and others of great illusion. What we must remember, however, is that each of these stories contains a little truth and that while the worlds of Faery and human can sometimes misunderstand each other, always, when each approaches the other with respect, love and an open heart, there is great magic to be found...the magic of the healing of the Earth.

Bridging the worlds of Faery and human, the light of the Earth and the land of our lives, bringing these two together, relights the fire in our lives. In letting magic kiss the mundane, we invite joy into our lives as once again we learn to hear the heartbeat of the Earth and stars, we find our Faery Hearts. Now we are strong on the land, we can choose to be strong in our vulnerable, open hearts again. Will you weave with me, with the others working and playing to build the bridges again? Will you weave with us the understanding of both worlds? Will you weave together the power on the land with the wonder of the Earth's heartbeat? Will you open to the possibility that to truly know the world, the whole world, is to know the mechanics and to understand the heart?

To be fey is a way of being.
Faery is the heart of life.
The fae are the spirits of the world.
Open, breathe, remember.
Sing with your Faery Heart...

Chapter 2

A Reason to Believe in Faeries

The Rationality of Irrationality

I believe in Faeries. That might seem a bit strange in our world of scientific rationality, but before you cast me aside as a lunatic, touched by the full moon that drives men mad, know that I am not mad, unless by madness you mean inspired. My muse sits on my shoulder tying knots in my hair and she whispers in my ear, filling my spirit, filling me with spirit. I like to talk in metaphors and the reason why will be made clear, so bear with me for a little while, hear me out. As you have picked up this book I know that you hear her call too, the song of the Queen of Faery who leads us to her realm through beauty and wonder, who enchants us into delighting in our lives and crafting something wondrous out of the world we have been gifted. If you have wondered why belief in the fae is fighting its way back into our culture despite the denial of anything beyond the physical, which is rampant in society, then perhaps I can enlighten you. This belief in all things Faery is quite rational. Let me show you why...

Some have argued that science is the highest goal of humanity, but I am hesitant to agree. Yes, science is an amazing tool. Science sheds light, brings wonders to view and generally enlightens us to the mechanics of the world. I am hesitant, however, because I do not believe that a tool should be our goal. Some have claimed that science is obviously a superior window to see the world through when compared to the holistic worldview of the Renaissance Magi who sought to attune to nature, for example. They say that, because we do not see many of these Magi anymore, while we have seen technology grow and grow, our understanding of the natural world has boomed through the practices of the sciences and we have more control over our world than ever before.

I am unsure that this is entirely true. Science is a brilliant tool for understanding the mechanics of the world; marvellous! But for understanding the whole world? When the world contains so much more than mechanics? What, you disagree? If you think the world is merely mechanical, then how can you hear my words when I am no longer speaking? Where is the sound of my voice, the sound of your thoughts? What are these thoughts that you think? These may have their roots in mechanical processes, sure, but can we really justify reducing the sphere of mental phenomena to mechanical processes when, as yet, we have not found a thought, when we cannot study emotions using science? We can look at the chemical and neurological processes that accompany thoughts and emotions, but this is not all that thought is. Take a look at a thought, what is the chemical formula for a thought of home? Which pattern in the brain is the thought? I'm not asking for what might cause the thought, but where the thought itself is. If the scientific view of the world cannot account for the realities of our mental and emotional lives, then perhaps it does not show the whole picture.

Not only has science not yet shown us what a thought and suchlike is, in its current mechanistic mode it cannot show us, for it does not know how to even begin studying thoughts. This is why we have multiple disciplines for studying the world; history studies elements of the past, psychology tries to explain our mental lives and sociology outlines and discusses movements of humans as social animals, for example. Our fascination with the tools of science has led us to try to describe these methodologies as sciences – pseudo-sciences, social sciences and so on – but while they try to reach an understanding of the parts of the world that they study, each of these disciplines is distinctly different from science and each other. To attempt to subsume them under our favourite model, science, is to deny that they do what science does not, cannot.

One might perhaps complain that I was confusing 'science' with 'natural science' and here I am using 'science' to refer to the mechanistic model of the natural sciences in order to draw out a point. When we want to show how objective, how true, our view is, we tend to try to justify our behaviour and explain the world in terms of 'science', by which we mean the natural sciences. Perhaps, however, we are mistaken in our reduction. I believe that the world is more than what can be explained by mechanistic processes and our attitude towards the world has a major impact on our understanding of it.

Science, we say ordinarily, seeks an understanding of the world. But what it really does is seek a mechanistic understanding of the world, which is fine when we are looking at the mechanics. This is not so fine when we come to live in the world.

A philosopher named Martin Heidegger draws to our attention the way in which, since technology has allowed us to, we have tended towards seeing the world as though everything that can be used as a resource is merely a resource and we lose any other understanding of it that we may have. Not treating beings in the world as the beings they are – say, not treating an oak tree as an oak tree in its own right – leads to our perspective of the world being diminished. An oak tree that is just wood ceases to have the emotional significance it may have had previously; we stop wondering what the Dryad of the tree might be thinking, what we can offer to her in return for the wood that we need and how our relationship with this particular tree sustains us. Once we stop seeing the world in terms of living beings that are interconnected, we begin to treat the world as though it is only a resource to be used for our own ends. Perhaps it is true that these are all mere resources, but look where this attitude, true or not, has gotten us.

Look at the world where our ecosystem depends on trees; trees producing oxygen and mopping up carbon dioxide, trees holding the soil together and re-fertilising it with their fruit and leaves, trees preventing the land from becoming parched desert, fit for nothing to grow. Look at the same world where we have decided to slash and burn whole forests to grow grain for beef, or where the forests are cut down for fancy furniture. Look at the world where we have designed a thing called 'the economy', which individuals are dependent upon in order to live and in many places round the world they starve to feed it.

In a world where we see everything as merely there to use, we have forgotten that everything is connected. We have forgotten that we will have to live, or die, with the consequences of killing forests to feed the economy, of putting resources above lives and of taking without much thought to what we might need to give back.

I propose an alternative. An old alternative. An alternative where we keep our understanding of the mechanics of the world, but where we also cultivate an understanding of the world that includes the notion of attuning with it and remembering that we are each a part of a living web, an ecosystem that stretches across the globe. I propose that 'understanding' cannot anymore, for practical reasons if no other, be reduced to a merely mechanistic framework. I propose that we need an understanding that includes the recognition of the world as more than mere matter, more than dead resource, more than something to be used. I propose, ultimately, that we cultivate an understanding of the world in which the world is alive.

I therefore propose that we invite the Faeries back into our lives.

The fae are spirits of nature, the essence of what it is to be a divine, living thing. Imagine if, instead of only looking at how the tree makes oxygen, we also thought about how the spirit of the tree was helping us to breathe, and how we helped it in return. We breathe with the trees. We needn't, it is true, resort to Faery tales in order to do this, it is possible to present the scientific explanation in a way that gets this idea across, but it lacks the mythological element we, as human beings, still connect to. Think of the stories, the adverts, the ways in which our societies build myths. And think of the ways we tap into them, we accept them, we take these stories and we tell them until they are true. We need only look at the magazines with their myths of 'beauty', or the stories that the media have told us of how the economy is in danger...maybe there was trouble on the horizon, but by accepting the story, we made it even more real, we stopped spending money because we thought there was a lack and this meant that the money stopped flowing, so now there is a lack.

Stories are powerful, and stories of the magic of the world speak to us on a deep level. We can re-learn to treat the world as though there were Faeries in every tree, as though they were watching us; learn to treat each part of the world as alive and full of spirit. Learning this, perhaps, would allow us to re-establish an equilibrium with the rest of the world, of which we are a part.

But, why Faeries?

Even if we accept that coming to terms with the world in the context of a story in which everything is alive and related would be a practical move, why Faeries?!

And, on top of this, can this kind of move really be healthy? Isn't this just a return to superstition of the Dark Ages?

To begin with the latter, for starters, what is wrong with superstition in itself? Many people have charms they count as lucky or rituals they follow superstitiously, which give meaning and pattern to their lives and overall help them to cope. What could be wrong with this? So long as we can hold both the scientific, rational understanding of the world that has allowed us to develop our technology so far and the superstitious understanding that can allow us to find a deeper meaning in our lives, keeping us happier and saner, why claim any intrinsic harm in superstition at all? In fact, one might want to ponder the superstitious power that the term 'science' has in our lives.

If we can find a story that allows us to live in a healthy

relationship with the world and each other, then surely this cannot be unhealthy. And, perhaps, a Faery story might be just the thing. An animistic story, where the spirits of nature will talk to us, work with us, help us, or play tricks when we're not being respectful; this kind of story might encourage us to treat the world around us with more respect. Given that disrespect of the natural world – by which I mean not treating it under its own terms and abusing it – does lead to difficulties, this story is even true.

Why, then, do I favour Faeries? In part, I've always been fascinated by them, but it runs deeper than that.

Faeries have long been held to be associated with the pure state of nature, where everything works together in relationship. The stories all talk about mutual respect (and the occasional stealing of cows, but then this theft often either results from the cows being on Faery land, the cow-owner disrespecting the land and its inhabitants or it leads to greater gifts for the 'victim' by the end of the tale) and give very specific rules for dealing with the fae, which translate very well into dealing with nature – such as not stealing, i.e., not taking what is not yours or not taking more than you need, and so on. Besides this, we have a degree of consensus on what Faeries actually are, how closely linked to the natural realm they are and what they are like. Most tales agree, for example, that they have particularly strict codes of honour, albeit often ones that seem odd to us!

If our reality is constructed through our experiences – and the relationships of things and meanings – and some individuals have experienced Faeries directly while others have experienced them through stories, and if Faeries have meaning for us, then why can't they be said to have a role within our world? Just like numbers have a role and a function in our world, or a song, constructed of nothing that looks like a song and yet is understood to be one, we have many things within our world for which we have no mechanistic explanation, which are not part of the mechanistic view. Faeries are not real under the mechanistic model, but in a mythological context, they have a definite reality; we understand what they are and, to a great extent, what role they have in human life. Throughout history, also, we have a great deal of agreement, up until recently, on the existence of the fae, our relationship to them, and the rough natures of the fae. If we are tempted to say that they cannot be real because only a few claim to experience them, then we need only glance at history to see that these people have a greater consensus than those who deny the existence of these beings.

Finally, to be honest, which kind of story is most important; a mechanistic reality, or a story that includes the mechanistic and allows us to live fully and healthily?

In short a belief in Faeries is perfectly reasonable in practical terms. If it is a helpful belief, a useful story, then why not consider it perfectly logical to believe in Faeries?

Besides, I like Faeries.

So, I believe that Faeries are important and now, I hope, you can see why.

But how, if they are so important, do we connect with them, find their world and find the part of ourselves that understands how to see and hear and talk to them?

The intention for this book is to explore these questions with you and to give you the keys to the answers. I will help you develop your relationships with the fae and your fey-side, the parts of you that you are, deep down, when you're truly honest with yourself and are not restricting yourself to roles you play in your daily life. At its core this book is about finding our Faery Hearts and opening them to the real magic in the world. And if you wonder what kind of magic I mean, go find a copy of Queen's song, A Kind of Magic and give it a listen. Magic is that sense of wonder and delight and truth in the world that they express so delightfully, and it leads to great transformations, which heal our souls and the worlds around us.

We will follow the music of the fae and the call of the Queen of Faery who knows that building bridges between the worlds is key to the survival of both realms. Remember always that the fae beings are the heart of nature – and thus wild, untamed, and potentially dangerous because we have no hold over them – and remember that if we approach with respect and work only with those who want to work with us, then we can begin to rediscover our own wild hearts, and this will open us to the magic in the world.

On this journey we are seeking the heart of Faery, in ourselves and in the world; we are seeking our Faery Hearts. Your Faery Heart is the part of yourself connected to the magic of the world, the part of you that is most natural, unrepressed and true to your essential self.

Your Faery Heart is important in many ways, since knowing yourself as you are before the roles you take on in your life gives you a point of reference for your actions, it helps you to recognise what you are comfortable with, which actions feed you in your life and which actions depress you. One key phrase to remember is 'joyful compassion'; it is important to have compassion for yourself and others, looking after yourself and not being deliberately mean to or neglectful of anyone. And it is important to live life as fully as you can, which is what I mean by joyfully. We may only get one chance at this, so let's live life like there is no tomorrow!

Your Faery Heart is a source inside you of great creativity and inspiration: sinking into the feeling of feyness puts you in a good place to create from, whether through visual arts, music, written pieces, baking or finding new solutions to problems. Any kind of creation can benefit from starting in this place, especially when balanced with technical ability! As you will see, to create from this state of being all you need to do is open your Faery Senses, breathe into your heart, and relax into magic and connection.

The feeling of connection that comes with the opening of your

Faery Heart is also good for healing, communication, and under-standing the world and others. Feeling the interconnectedness of everything shows you where you belong in the world, and how you are an important part of nature, just like the bee that buzzed by last summer, the star that heats our whole planet, the cliffs slowly crumbling into the sea. Everything has its place, and each is as important as any other.

This is why we seek the Faery Heart within ourselves. It is a state of being, a way of living, in which we are who we are and in which we connect deeply to the magic of Faery. This allows us to find far more joy in our lives than we ever thought possible. When we fill our lives with joy it spills over into the world; by enchanting ourselves in this way we enchant the world and bring healing to both Faery and human lands.

Chapter 3

Why Walk this Path to Faeryland?

The Thoughts Behind this Faery Path

If we look at the stories of Faeries, all the myths and legends, we see a common theme; they are all very strongly connected to, or embodying, nature. They are not, however, merely the plants or trees or forces they embody, they are beings that are inherently magical, beyond limits. Faeries are natural magic and, as part of nature ourselves, the magic within us is fey.

Humans are lured into Faeryland by beauty. Beautiful music, beautiful visions, beautiful food. And this beauty, once we return to Earth, we pine for. So Faeryland is that place within the world, and ourselves as part of nature, in which the sense of magic, wonder and beauty lies, the natural core of our being. The heart of the world we reach through connecting to our Faery Heart.

If our hearts, at their untamed core, are places of beauty and magic, then following the call to Faeryland will open our hearts again to the beauty of the world. If we learn to touch the fey parts of ourselves then we can move through our lives open to the beauty that surrounds us and so we can reconnect to the natural world, with the other beings on the Earth as our brothers and sisters and kin.

When we find our Faery Heart we find the bridge to the other world where magic lives. By opening to the beauty of the world we will learn both how to find that beauty wherever we go and how to create a more wonder-filled life. In uncovering our true self from the layers of expectations and restrictions placed upon us by our daily life we will discover what it is we truly desire and what truly makes us happy. In doing so we can choose to transform our life into what we long for it to be. This process of finding our true self is the key to all magic and magic, at its core, is healing for ourselves and for the world. Once we know who we are and what of our lives we choose to change – and how we'd choose to change them – we can begin to rewrite the stories of our lives into something that fills us with delight. This is not purely a selfish act either; healed, whole, happy and healthy we are able to carry that into the world around us. In finding the magic of Faery within yourself you can then begin to share it with those around you, helping them to find the beauty and joy in their own lives. It is like filling yourself with so much joy that it spills over and touches all those around you – healing the world one wonder-filled heart at a time.

If we are true to ourselves we are happy. If we are happy, we can help others to be happy too. This is the gift the Faeries have given me to give to you, a path to your own delight, in your own Faery Heart, from which, together, we can fill our lives with joy and heal those around us by re-enchanting the world, bringing back the magic, wonder, connection and delight that we most often remember from the innocence of childhood.

And, of course, we recall the other parts of the stories of the fae...the wilder parts...the dangerous parts... They are untamed and not human and so their ethics are a little less strict than ours tend to be. In our heart we are natural beings, just like them; we have learnt really wonderful human skills, such as compassion and language, but in our search for order we have tried to tame our essential Selves and instead we have locked them away. These parts of ourselves hurt, so each day we die a little inside.

Here we choose to walk down a path that will lead us back to the parts within us that hold who we truly are. We seek all our parts, those that are good at communication, at compassion, and those that are good at standing up for us and being free. We do not have to give up the gifts of humanity in order to find our Faery Hearts and heal our lives, we can free ourselves of those things that do not serve us, release those things that hold us back and fly, carrying both gifts of humanity and gifts of Faery. We can choose to be both human and wild. That is what it means to be fey.

Fey means free. Free of the locks we've used to keep ourselves acceptable and free to choose to move in compassion and beauty. Fey means to be free to be our real Selves, to live our lives without unhealthy compromises, to dance to Faery music so we are filled with love and joy and deep feelings of connection even in a business meeting or on a busy, grimy underground train.

Fey means so full of shiny, happy, beauty, that you cannot help but share it.

We look for our hearts and when we live with them open, in the world, we are not only happier in ourselves, but we share some of that light with everyone around us. We need to be true to ourselves, and we need to live with others. I believe, with all my heart, that being true to ourselves will help us to live with others in love and joy.

The world is getting greyer by the day. Look at the people around you. I hope they are happy, and I fear they are not. Our world needs a resurgence of open hearts, shared beauty and joy. So let us join those that already search for their hearts. Let us walk this path into Faery so that we can return with our hearts and fill the world with colour again!

Let our nights be full of beauty,
Let our days be full of light,
Let our wings spread out to touch the stars
Let our feet walk the way that's right.

A prayer sings in our heart as the alarm clock wakes us; we wait, for just a moment on the edge of sleep, warm and safe, dreams close by…

Our eyes open just a crack and the light seeps in, sunlight pouring through the chink in the curtains.

We realise, in that moment before we surrender to the reality that we must arise and wash and work and go about our day, that what would make this day more beautiful, more ours, is having a little space to let our hearts peek out, seep out into the world like the sunshine filters in. We decide, in that moment, to make space for our hearts in our lives.

Chapter 4

Preparing for the Journey

The secret of the journey to find your Faery Heart is that you carry your Heart with you – like Dorothy in the Wizard of Oz, who finds the magic that will take her home in the ruby slippers she has worn the whole time, your Faery Heart is always with you. The journey is still necessary, however, as it takes a change in perspective to be able to see what is hidden. We've learnt to hide our Faery Hearts, but we can still catch glimpses of them even now. Using trance and trust we shall begin the work of finding ourselves where we are, right now. Along our path we will learn more about ourselves, gain new skills and return again and again to finding ourselves where we are at each point along the path. Each step will show us more of what we carry within us.

Exercise 1. Gathering Your Travel Kit
Here I offer you a selection of tools you might like to gather for your journey – a heart-box to represent your Faery Heart and a Faery altar to help you to make space for Faery in your life, a mirror to show you your true Faery Heart, a travel-journal to record your adventures and materials for a deck of cards that will be both snapshots of your discoveries and windows into the past, present and future. These are all simply suggestions, things that will be played with later in your journey and need not be found right away. Nothing here must be expensive either, find things that make you smile on all levels and don't worry about perfection – happy imperfection is the crack that lets the magic into the world!

Each of these items is useful in your explorations of Faery-Hearted magic, and they are also reminders to your subconscious and a demonstration to your fey self and fae guides that you are committed to this path. This encourages your subconscious to take it seriously and support you in this adventure and it shows respect to the Faery beings who can help you, which they appreciate and respond well to.

The Faery Altar

If we want to know our true, fey, hearts and to let them shine into the world, then we need to make space for them in our lives. One good way to do this is to find or make a Faery altar. An altar is a physical space that contains representations of what you wish to honour in your life. A Faery altar is, then, a space where you can keep reminders of the beauty, wonder and magic of Faery.

Choose a corner in your home that can become a dedicated space for an altar. It can be a shelf, a table, a corner, a box you look in every day, a candle you light in a beautiful candle holder, a jar full of shinies, a statue, a mobile, a bowl of pebbles, a picture on the wall or whatever resonates for you. Gather together objects that remind you that the world is full of magic and that Faeries live just out of sight. Over time you can add to your altar, changing the objects there according to how you feel as your journey progresses. It needn't be obvious to anyone but you what this space is – this is just for you and the fae.

A good object to start with is a candle. Flames act as points you can focus on, they keep the energy in a space moving and fresh and they light the way for you to see the path ahead. You might also choose something to represent the world tree, a huge, beautiful tree that bridges the worlds of human, Faery and other spirits. An image or statue of a tree, or perhaps a small decorated branch you find while exploring a place that feels magical or special could represent the world tree. The world tree can help you cross between the worlds of the everyday and the magical and it can act as a reminder of the natural world that surrounds us and in which the heart of Faery can be found. As we are building better relationships between ourselves and the magical, natural realm it is important to choose your items carefully. Try to avoid harming plants or animals while you collect things for your altar. The energy you put into being mindful of the new relationship you wish to create will show the Faery beings that you are reaching out in a respectful and genuine way – this will show them that you are worth connecting with and helping on your path. The Faery altar also gives them a place to call home in your living space, welcoming those beings to take a more active role in guiding you.

The Heart-Box

On this journey we are seeking our Faery Hearts and a useful tool for this is the heart-box.

Find yourself a heart-box; some kind of small box that you can put things into and take things out of to explore what is in your heart during your journeys to and from Faeryland. You can start with something plain if you like, in a shape that warms your heart and then slowly decorate it and fill it with things representing what is in your heart. Your heart-box can be any kind of container in any shape that makes you happy. It can be store-bought, found or made. If you prefer, you can also use a bag or a cloth wrap, like the old Irish crane bag of Manannan MacLir or the medicine bundles of shamans in many cultures.

Choose or design your heart-box, this space for your heart in your life. The heart-box is similar to an altar but more private, it is a reminder and a way of honouring what you find on this path. Because your heart is always changing, the contents and perhaps the decorations of your heart-box will be constantly shifting, but it should always reflect what you know of your true fey self.

An altar is a focal point for your magical work in the world – and make no mistake, this is magical – and your heart-box is a reflection of the things you love, the things you want to love, the things in your heart that scare you, the things that thrill you.

Because it is more private, a container that can be closed, your heart-box is a safe place for the secrets in your heart.

This is just for you, you need never explain it to anyone else, this is a safe space for you to feel whatever you feel. Gift yourself with as much time as you need to explore your heart. You have a whole lifetime and you do not need to find even one thing to put in your heart-box just yet. Many people have ignored their hearts for a long time and it takes a while before they are able to let go of the stresses that keep them from seeing. Others try too hard or have something specific in mind. Just let whatever comes to you come. For now, open to finding a suitable container for making space in your life to explore your heart. Later on our path you will work with the heart-box to discover the truth of your Faery Heart.

The Magic Mirror

Remember the magic mirror in Snow White? The Queen had a magic mirror that could only show the truth. She was very vain and each morning she would ask it: 'Mirror, mirror, on the wall, who is the fairest of them all?' Each morning, in response, it would show her the most beautiful lady in the kingdom. The trouble came when she saw someone who was not her, Snow White, and was jealous. In this way the magic of the truthful mirror revealed what kind of person the Queen was. All Faery tales contain sparkles of truth and magic mirrors really do exist. They can be used to see the truth about yourself, when approached in the right way.

I recommend finding a small mirror as this will be invaluable for future magical explorations. It is almost impossible to see yourself without a mirror and they are perfect for looking at both your body and your spirit. In order to find your Faery Heart you must be able to see yourself clearly and a mirror lets you do this.

The best kind of mirror is one you can hold in your hand and fit in your pocket. Folding compact mirrors are great since they have a cover that protects the surface of the mirror while you travel. You can also open a compact mirror and pretend to be checking for a stray eyelash when really you are checking in with your Faery Heart!

Again, your mirror can be ornate or plain. You can use a cheap mirror as effectively as an expensive one (and if you want to use a cheap mirror for now and save up for something gloriously ornate then that's fine too). With magical tools it is important that you are happy with them and that you hold the intention for it to be special. The magic is not in the mirror, it is in you. Every time you use your mirror, however, it will collect a little magic until it becomes an enchanted object itself. When this happens it can support you in your explorations by tapping into the magic it holds for you.

Once you have found your mirror, set it aside from everyday use and keep it for Faery magic only. If it does not have a lid or a cover, then make a little bag or a cover for it. Each time you uncover it to use it, perhaps you might like to say a few magic words as a spell to enchant it further and to put yourself in the right frame of mind! Here is a charm that you can use, or be inspired by to create your own:

Mirror, mirror, in my hand,
Blessed by light from Faeryland,
Reveal that which I need to see,
Show the truth of me to me.

A Travel Journal

The magic of Faery is subtle and can slip from our memories swiftly under the glaring light of daily life, so somewhere to record your adventures and insights, feelings and thoughts, visions and musings is really helpful. This can be as ornate as a book hand-bound with wood or leather and containing handmade paper, or a simple as loose leaves in a binder. The important thing is not the journal itself, but that you keep a record of those moments of beauty and magic so you can remind yourself of them when life encourages you to forget. Sometimes you can only see the patterns long after the event, so it is good to be able to look back over your journey and discover the connections you missed at the time. It is sometimes better to have something that is not too precious as you need to feel comfortable enough to use your journal; you need something that you can feel completely free to play with.

In your journal you can write, paint, draw, doodle, collage, finger paint, stick photos or whatever else you enjoy doing to record your thoughts and feelings. After each exercise in this book and at any other moment you like, make some time to record what is going on for you. Later you can look back over your musings and remember the magic you have found...and see how far you have come!

Today, just grab any paper and any pen or pencil to scribble down how you are feeling right now. How do you feel about what you have read so far? Are you excited? Nervous? Curious? Delighted? As you gather together your travel kit, make a note of what you collect, what you're thinking and how you feel about it all so that further down the path you can remember what you might otherwise forget. Later, if you like, you can find beautiful books and binders, but for today any paper is perfect.

Oracle Cards

Personally, alongside my travel journal, I like to make cards for explorations, inspirations, and memories so that I have a deck of cards, ever evolving, with which I can further explore what I discover. I often make these cards as collages, photos or paintings, which I scan and then shrink down to print out a copy at playing card size for ease of shuffling. If you are of an artistic temperament, or even if not, perhaps you might like to draw, paint, doodle, write or collage cards for your own ever-evolving deck of memories, experiences and inspirations. I suggest cards because they are tactile, they feel good to hold, and they are portable. And, most importantly, they allow you to shuffle the things you record and lay them out to discover new connections between your discoveries. I use a standard playing card size, 2.5 inches by 3.5 inches, but you might want something a bit bigger depending on your preferred method of play...or you can make huge sprawling collections of posters and sticky-notes all over your walls. Follow your own heart here, as always.

To Make Your Own Deck

Cut pieces of card to a size that you find easy to hold and to shuffle. These are the bases for your cards.

Breathe deeply and relax.

Hold a question, a feeling or an idea in your mind.

Using whatever art materials you feel most drawn to, begin to play.

Stop when you are ready and admire your new card!

Once you've finished each card spend a little bit of time musing on the image that arose – what does this card have to tell you about yourself?

You can also make your images using the same technique, but in whatever size you choose. Then photograph and upload or scan them into your computer and print them out at the size you wish your cards to be.

Using Oracle Cards

Oracle cards are useful for when you are looking for clarity or direction. Breathe deeply and relax. Hold your question in your mind and shuffle the deck. Pull cards from the deck, one at a time until you feel you have enough – one may feel like enough, or perhaps five or six cards are calling to you. Lay out the cards in front of you, face up, and see what story the pictures make when you look at them. If you have one card: what is the main image in the card? If you have several: how do they connect with each other? What do they have in common? See how you feel about the content of the cards, and what they remind you of. Write any insights down, the pattern may become clearer further down the path...

If you do not want to make your own deck, you can always choose a readymade oracle deck of some kind. I have created a deck called *The FeyHearted Oracle*, based on my work with the fae, which you can get directly from myself, or you may like Brian Froud's *Faery Oracle*. You can also use tarot, rune-stones, ogham sticks or other divination tools in similar ways.

The Heart Layout

Oracle cards are often laid out in specific patterns to tell certain kinds of stories about our lives. Some map out past-present-future, others tell tales of the forces in our lives. I developed this card layout in order to help us figure out where we are in ourselves and how much in tune with our heart our lives are. You can use any form of divination cards, sticks or stones that call to you. The idea is to pull three oracle cards, one for each of the words in the phrase 'I Am Here' and lay them in the shape of a heart, or a downward pointing triangle.

'I' represents your core, the state of your heart now, and/or what is in your heart right now.

'Am' represents how you are expressing your heart.

'Here' represents your life and situation, the state of the world around you.

Once you have the cards, turn them over and contemplate them, meditate with them, read them however you find best. Play a little. See what they say to you about each part, your essence, your expression, and your life situation. See if they are working together or in balance, or if something needs to shift.

Then pull a fourth card and lay it to the right of the others.

This card is called 'Changing'.

This card is either that which needs to change in order for the first three points to come into balance, or, if they are already in balance, it points to the next movement, the next cycle, the next direction to keep in balance, in flow.

Now read the fourth card in relation to the first three and contemplate.

Write down all your thoughts, the cards you choose and any insights. Leave a little space next to what you've written and come back after a week or two to reflect on the reading again; do you have any further insights to add to your notes?

Be honest with yourself to get the most out of this exercise.

Exercise 2. Trance

In the search for our Faery Heart we will make use of trance, in fact, if you have been following the directions and suggestions so far you have already been using trance! Trance is simply a more receptive way of being than our everyday mode, to move into trance means to naturally change your brain waves into those normally reserved for sleeping, dreaming, or deep relaxation, which allows communication between the heart and mind to happen. The simplest method is to focus gently on your breathing.

Relax and pay attention to your breath as it flows in and out of your body.

Feel your muscles relax a little more with each breath out, feel your mind calm.

Imagine a golden light flowing round you, washing away tension, soothing muscles and mind, filling you with soft warmth.

Relax into the feeling of calm and breathe steadily and deeply, but gently.

Imagine that all the beauty of the world is around you

right now and every breath in draws that beauty into your body, warming and filling it with joy.

Imagine that every breath out takes tensions from your body and allows you to relax a little more.

Take your time with this, practise breathing in the beauty around you, and breathing out the tensions within you, relaxing more with each breath. With practise, this can be done anywhere, anywhen.

The key to trance is calming the worries and insistent thoughts that run riot in your mind normally, and relaxing. The easiest way to do this is through repetition, like concentrating on your breathing as above, or something like knitting, swaying, a simple dance step that you repeat, or listening to a beat that repeats over and over. It takes time to sink into trance at first, but with practise it gets quicker and you can go deeper into the trance state. Trance is a continuum. From our normal consciousness right into sleep, our state of mind and body gradually changes. Trance is consciously choosing to relax the mind and body without sleeping, while remaining aware and opening to inspiration – the influx of spirit. Over time you can learn to relax more, go deeper and deeper into trance states, and be more open to your subconscious mind and the other worlds.

Returning From Trance and Grounding

Coming out of trance properly is important, otherwise you can spend days feeling spaced out, which, personally, makes me irritable when trying to deal with everyday events. When you finish your trance, then drink a glass of water and make notes on anything you want to remember; however clearly you think you'll remember it later making some kind of record will really help! Get completely back into your body and leave thinking about what you experienced for an hour or two, or more. This is often called 'grounding' or 'getting grounded' because you come back to earth and release the excess energy into it! Some easy ways to ground include:

- Saying your name aloud three times
- Patting the edges of your body
- Wiggling your toes and feeling the earth beneath you
- Getting up and doing something mundane, like going home and doing the washing up
- Talking to another human being about mundane things
- Eating something crunchy and starchy, especially as trance is hungry work

Exercise 3. Grounding as a Tree

As embodied beings we have the gift of physical existence, ensuring that our spirit is aligned with our physical body makes life much easier. Grounding brings our spirits back to earth when we've been in a trance and it reconnects us to the Earth – our home. One technique for grounding that many folk employ is to stand up and imagine that you are a tree:

Imagine that you are a tree with your roots reaching deep into the ground while bending over and allowing your fingers to touch the floor, and then straighten up with a smooth motion and stretch up to the sky while imagining your branches reaching up to the sky. Bring your arms down slowly and take a deep breath into your centre. Feel your body, strong and supported by the Earth and connected to the sky.

Protection and Cleansing

In all the work we do we are polishing up our hearts and letting them shine a little brighter; we are opening up to more energy, more light, more life. There are many reasons we learn to close down in the first place and one of those reasons is to hide ourselves from the energies that are not ours, which get stuck to us. Think back to a time when you were in a place or around a person who made you feel uncomfortable, even though their behaviour was fine. When you left the situation, did you feel like some of that ickiness had stuck to you? Did you find yourself wanting to shake something off, or feel like you needed to shower to get clean again? This is because you've picked up some of that dirty energy, which will then weigh you down. The same can happen with people you are comfortable with when they are upset, you can easily pick up and carry that unhappy energy for them, which will then interfere with your life. There are simple ways of dealing with those energies, however, and they boil down to energetic cleanliness and protection.

When you are about to do some work that will open you up, or before you go into a situation where there will be other people or energies that you know you will be susceptible to, you can create a protective bubble to keep you safe. Before working magically in a space, or after interacting with others, you can wash away those bits of energy that do not belong to you.

Exercise 4. Cleansing Techniques
Every magical and religious tradition has some form of space and personal cleansing, and they often involve clean water:

> Take a bowl of clean water and a pinch of salt. Hold the salt in your palm and imagine it filling with bright, golden-white light. Add the salt to the water and stir it in, imagining that, as it does, the salt transforms the water into cleansing light. Now dip your fingers into the water and flick it around the room, making sure you get it into each corner and in the centre, watching as the drops of light-filled water cleanse the space. Flick it over yourself and feel it cleaning away any energy that is not yours. Salt is particularly good, but you can also use other herbs in the water, rose water, or just water on its own, which you visualize filling with golden-white light.

You can also do a similar thing using a shower, by visualizing that the water is full of light and it is washing your energy clean at the same time as cleansing your body.

Smudging is another popular method, where a dried herb, usually white sage, is burnt and the smoke is wafted around the space and the person to be cleansed. Like the water, the smoke is visualized as cleansing the energy of the space and person. I use British sage for smudging and a local owl feather, which I collected myself, as that is where I'm based. Mugwort is said to be a good Anglo-Saxon cleansing herb, and it also encourages dreams and visions. I have also used whatever incense is to hand. Frankincense works well (and smells lovely), but needs a special censor to burn properly and avoid setting fire to yourself or your space.

Experiment with cleansing using smoke and water techniques. You will find that you can ask the plant and water fae to help with activities like cleansing but, as always, as long as you approach these activities with a sense of respect then the spirits will support you and teach you.

Exercise 5. Protective Light

Once your space and self are clean, a protective circle acts like a coat to keep the etheric mud off your freshly washed self. You can use amulets to protect you, certain stones or herbs and so on carried in a pocket or hung around your neck are useful, but the simplest and most effective way is to visualize yourself surrounded by the golden-white light, already encountered in the trance exercise, with the intention that it will protect you.

Try this:

Cleanse your space and yourself with one of the techniques listed previously.

Stand or sit comfortably and allow your breathing to become slow and deep.

Relax and allow your bones to support your muscles in an upright position.

Breathe into relaxation.

Feel the ground beneath you and the sky above you.

Imagine a golden-white light beginning to gather around you, becoming brighter and brighter with each breath. It fills the space around you in an egg shape, large enough that you can stretch your arms out to either side and still be just within the light.

That light glows strong and clear around you, burning away any negativity you feel and wish to let go of.

Know that nothing can harm you whilst you are surrounded by this light.

Now, as you breathe, imagine the edges of that light becoming more solid, like a membrane that covers the outside of the light in an egg shape around you.

Know that you can see out through that membrane, but that nothing can enter through it without your permission.

Allow the light to fade from your vision, but feel it still present, a protective bubble of power.

Get up and engage in some everyday things, periodically checking in with that egg of golden light. If it begins to feel less strong you can breathe some more light into it and strengthen it again.

Practise this until you can conjure up the light egg with only a few breaths and a moment to visualize it.

Visualisation

Visualisation is another skill you may wish to develop. It means to imagine something so strongly it feels like it is there. Use all your senses; imagine the sound, the smell, the texture, the colours, even the taste. One sense may be easier than others, and you may find that your strongest sense is the sense of knowing. The clearer you visualise something, the more it can affect you, the more easily it can become ensouled by spirit, filled with life. A visualisation can take on a life of its own and, at that point, you know it's no longer you that is driving it, but that magic moves through it.

The reason for the journeys in this book is to relax your mind into the trance state, the state where it can receive information, and to visualise a setting to tell the world what information you are looking for is. Relax into the journey and imagine it is true, soon you'll find things within your imagination acting with a life of their own, and then you know there is more than your conscious mind at work. Be they messages from your subconscious, your own heart, or from the fey world of the heart of nature, the more you trance into Faeryland, the more you begin to touch the fey heart of yourself and the world.

Exercise 6. Visiting your Dream-Temple

You can practise visualization by creating yourself a safe space in the dream-realms of your heart. Over time the place you imagine becomes independent and lives on its own, a sacred place in the dreamworlds beyond the mundane for you to start your journeys in. When we dream, daydream or imagine things, we access this dream-realm. Visualisation is imagining with intent and intent allows us to shape our inner landscape to our desires. Because this is a safe and sacred space in the dreamland of your heart, I like to call this your dream-temple, though it may not look like any temple you'd recognize as such. Here, then, is a guided meditation that uses trance and visualization to discover your dream-temple. To use a guided meditation such as this, read it through once to get a sense of what will be asked of you, and then you can ask someone to read it through for you to listen to, you can record it in your own voice and listen to the recording, go through it from memory or read it through with softened gaze and visualize what you are reading as you read it.

Begin by settling somewhere comfortable.

Notice the world around you, above you, below you, before you, behind you and beside you. This orientates you, honours the land you are living in and reminds you that magic is all around you in the beauty of the world that extends in all directions.

Close or soften your eyes and feel your centre, feel the weight of your body and your centre of gravity in your belly.

Breathe deeply and imagine the golden light surrounding you.

Imagine that with every breath you breathe in beauty and breathe out tension.

Allow your mind to relax.

Now, with your mind's eye, imagine you can open your eyes and see the dream-realms of your heart. This is the place your heart dreams of.

Allow your imagination to settle on the kind of landscape that makes your heart happiest.

Imagine walking through this landscape until you come to a specific place that makes you feel safe. Perhaps it is a garden, perhaps a castle, perhaps a grove in a forest or a lake or a cave. Whichever place comes to you that feels like home is right.

Explore your dream-temple.

When you are ready, breathe deeply and retrace your steps back, out of the place you have found.

Feel yourself returning to your body more with each breath.

Make notes on your journey, describe the landscape, your dream-temple and any troubles you may have had with this exercise.

Repeat this at least once a week until your dream-temple feels like somewhere that exists when you are not there. Experiment then with travelling there using different paths; can you find it by breathing into your heart and feeling yourself arrive? Can you change parts of it, growing new plants or creating new structures perhaps? Take as long as you like each time and return to your dream-temple often.

You can visit your dream-temple for healing, for quiet, for space to think or space to play. Every time you visit it, you practise your powers of visualization and your ability to move into trance as well as giving it more power. This can be your home in the dream-worlds, your spirit-temple or simply a peaceful garden to give yourself a time out when life gets tough. Remember to write down your experiences each time, and to come back to your body each time – get grounded!

Chapter 5

Honesty and the Second Sight

Music calls you.

Gently, insistently, just beyond the edges of your hearing, beautiful music.

The softest voice whispers in your heart, saying, 'Now is the time.'

You catch yourself halfway out the door, your feet followed your heart before your mind realised there was a journey to take.

Grab your coat, pick up a mirror, and walk with me.

We go to find our true hearts; we go to find the heart of Faery.

Thomas the Rhymer is an old Scottish tale of a real person who travelled to Faeryland and came back with greater gifts than anyone could have expected.

Once upon a time there was a gentleman called Thomas who fell asleep under a hawthorn tree, which is known to be beloved of the Faeries. When he awoke a lady stood before him who was so beautiful he thought she was the Queen of Heaven! The lovely lady told him that, in fact, she was the Queen of Faeryland and she invited him to travel with her on her fine steed.

It was a long journey across rivers of blood, which roared like the sea, but finally they arrived in her country. There she warned him to only eat food she gave him and to remain silent for the time he stayed. Seven years he served her faithfully, silent and loving. After seven years she returned him to the mortal world and, in return for his faithful service, she gifted him with the Tongue that Cannot Lie.

Because he could only speak truly, everything he said came true.

Thomas became known as 'True Thomas', he was a great poet who made prophecies until the day that he disappeared, returning to the Faery Court of his Queen who he loved dearly. Now True Thomas lives in Faeryland, though he sometimes returns to help other people who wish to make the journey or to bring the magic of Faery back into the world as he knows the ways between the worlds better than any human living on the green land of Earth.

Since you wish to travel a Faery path, he has come with a challenge for you:

> *True Thomas asks you for a promise of truth.*
> *This path requires honesty.*
> *Can you commit to being as honest with yourself as you are able?*
> *If you cannot, or will not, then no matter what this path can show you, you will not see it.*

Keeping his word kept him safe in his travels through unknown lands, and speaking only the truth meant that he could foretell the future. From Thomas' gifts from Faery we learn that our words are powerful and honesty more powerful still. There is magic in what we say, magic in the stories we tell. We have told ourselves stories that keep us small and dependent on a culture that rolls towards self-destruction. If we speak honestly then the stories we tell will come to pass.

We can change our worlds by telling new stories. If you always look at the things you love and say, 'I cannot', then you never will, but if you look at what you love and change your story, if you tell yourself, 'I can', then possibilities open up to you and you will find a way. At the same time, we do have limitations. Honesty with ourselves means that we recognize the limitations we truly have and the limitations we think we have – and we can tell the difference.

At each point in our journeys we are able to see different things clearly. If, at each moment, we are as honest as we can be we have the chance to see which limitations are real, and which we can surpass. When we see honestly, we can change our stories accordingly. We cannot make ourselves fly unaided by saying we can – these are not limitations we can break – and so to say so teaches our heart to stop trusting our mouth.

To make this journey, where we know our Faery Hearts and change our stories to those that are enchanted, we must learn to be honest with our words. This is why True Thomas asks us for an oath of honesty. When we learn to rewrite our own stories in accordance with our true desires, we craft a life of wonder; this work is the greatest spell of all, a lifetime built on the magic of knowing our hearts and making our wishes come true.

Exercise 7. True Thomas' Oath of Honesty

Sit at your altar and, if you can, light a candle to represent the flames that light your path and carry magic between the worlds.

Ask, out loud if you can, for the Queen of Faery and True Thomas to witness your oath. Use whatever words come from your heart, they can be as simple as, 'I invite the Queen of Faery and True Thomas to witness my oath.'

Hold your magic mirror and breathe softly, deeply. Allow your mind to calm and let yourself to sink into a light trance.

Look into your eyes in the mirror, breathe deeply and ask yourself if you are ready to be completely honest with yourself. If not, ask how honest you are able to be with yourself.

And then make a promise, to yourself, witnessed by True Thomas and the Faery Queen, to be as honest with yourself as you are able on this path.

Allow the words to rise up from your heart. You can choose your own words in the moment, write an oath before you start or you can use these words if you'd prefer: *'True Thomas, you who walked the way to Faeryland before me, I ask you to witness my commitment to honesty on this path. I promise to be truthful in my journey to the heart of Faery within myself and in the world. I promise to always strive for honesty so that I may know myself and so my words become true and what I say must be, must be.'*

Breathe into your heart.

Allow any sense of response that might come to arise in your heart and mind.

When you are ready, thank the Faery Queen and True Thomas for their presence and return to yourself.

Record your experience and ground yourself.

If you ever feel unsure of where you're headed on this path you can always ask Thomas the Rhymer, as a human who has walked the paths between Faeryland and the human world, for guidance. Thomas knows the paths between the worlds and has been known to help seekers of the Faery Heart. To contact him you can sit at your altar with the candle lit or outside somewhere quiet, breathe deeply, relax and say a prayer for guidance.

Here are some words to get you started, but the best prayers are those that come straight from the heart with true feeling:

Prayer to Thomas the Rhymer
Dear Thomas, you who walked the paths,
Betwixt between and back again,
I walk with you through wax and wane
Please show to me my way.

The Gift of the Faery Queen
The day begins, the sun dawns, the light streams into the world. We have decided to make space for our heart, for Faery, and in making this choice our heart has opened, just a little, but perhaps we're unsure.

At work, at school, moving through the world we live our everyday life in, we find ourselves wondering just how we can see what belongs in our heart, and what can be left behind, or kept only as a useful mask or tool, to wear and use, but not to become too attached to.

We remember the stories, the stories of Faery.

We remember our childhood walks, the moments where, maybe, just on the edge of our vision, we would catch a glimpse of the fey ones, shining and soft, sharp and powerful, caring and dangerous and ever so wild, Oh! Always, ever so, ever so wild!

And we realise… Who else could help us find our wild Faery Hearts but the ever-beautiful Queen of the Faeries?

The moment comes upon you, sneaks up on you, dances towards you silently like an invisible sacred temple dancer…the moment when you realise you can hear her voice. Her voice, calling you. The Faery Queen. She remembers you. She wants you to come home. She waits for you.

It is your choice, now, she offers an invitation. Will you answer?

Today, choose.

Will you follow the Faery Queen's song?

Will you accept her invitation to see with Faery Senses, to see the untamed beauty of the world, to see to the heart of things?

Exercise 8. Awakening the Second Sight

Choose, and, as soon as you can, take a walk. Search out somewhere that feels like magic, full of delight and a sense of wildness. I went to the edge of a forest, you might go to the top of a mountain, or to a fountain in the middle of your city, or maybe catch a train and watch the fields swish by.

Find somewhere that feels *right*.

Visualise that golden, protective egg around you.

Breathe deeply as you walk, really feel your feet on the ground, really notice the world around you.

Breathe it all in.

Take a walk with the intention of opening to the fae.

Say with your footsteps, 'Faery Queen, I accept!'

Lay out a biodegradable offering, one which will not damage the world the Faeries love; biscuits, milk and honey, flowers made from rice paper, your favourite drink, a song sung to the wind, a dance, a picture burnt to ash…a gift for the Faery Queen, given freely and with love and trust, to thank her for her invitation, her help, her blessing.

And call to the Faery Queen, ask her to open your eyes, to wake you up, to show you how to open your eyes to Faery yourself.

Breathe deeply and let yourself open.

If you are unsure, or not ready, then accept this and promise yourself you will return when you are ready.

But, if you breathe deep, truly ready, she will open your Faery eyes, open your heart, and let you see beyond the mundane world. She will give you the gift of Faery Sight – sight that is more than normal sight, sight that is feeling and knowing and reaching into the magic of Faery.

All you need do is ask.

Feel your heart open, like a flower, like wings unfurling, like a sunrise.

Breathe in.

Feel yourself open, expand, and let the sensations at the edge of your normal experience in.

Open to the fae in the world and see what you see, hear, smell, taste, feel, know…

When you are ready to return let yourself close down and come back to normal consciousness, record your experiences and ground yourself.

If you feel that you have not been successful, come back to try again another day. Maybe you could use an oracle to ask for clues as to why you feel that way and what might be required of you to succeed next time. Give yourself plenty of time to experience the slow, subtle opening of Faery Sight, Faery Senses. At first it might be almost unnoticeable, but each time you open your heart and ask to be opened it will become stronger and easier. Read further and come back to this exercise, as with all the exercises in this book, as often as you feel you should until you find that the Faery Sight comes so easily to you it is like breathing.

Turning the Sight on Our Selves

The Faery Queen has given you the gift of Faery Sight and gifts are not made to sit on a shelf and gather dust. Gifts are given to be used.

But, we wonder, how are we to use this gift? We sit in our human world and puzzle over this beautiful, inhuman gift, sparkling in our Selves and we begin to understand that it can show us both the fae without, and the fey within.

When I say Faery Sight I'm talking about opened senses, whichever sense or senses that light up in you. It may be sight, or it may be hearing or touch, or it may be knowing, an ability to sense beyond the human world. Each person is unique and so we all open in different ways.

Learning how to open our Faery Senses has two key uses:

- Opening us to the wild magic and beauty of the world, the realm of Faery.
- Allowing us to truly see ourselves.

How can we turn our Faery Senses on ourselves? How exactly do we use this gift to reveal our heart to us? Sensing the fae without is one thing that perhaps sounds easy and we will come to that soon. But the fey within? The easiest answer is that this takes meditation. Lots of it. You can sit in meditation with your Faery Senses opened in the way the Faery Queen showed you, and focus on yourself. This works. There are also other ways, ways that are inspired by processes such as Soulcollage™ and Soul

Journaling and all the imaginative ways people have explored their many selves.

Compassion, Courage and Stories

While gazing into the depths of your heart and exploring what belongs there you will find things that you were not expecting and things that you've chosen to pretend don't belong. The stories we learn as we grow up encourage us to deny many parts of our true hearts and, when we learn what those stories are, we can learn to rewrite them. The process of discovering these stories can be painful, however, so we need to have compassion for ourselves. If we can walk this path with self-love then we can take care of ourselves and grow in healthy ways.

Even though it can be painful, understanding the stories we have learned and taken into ourselves as true allows us to change them. Our stories keep us in particular roles and sometimes those roles are harmful to us – not always because they are bad, however, sometimes it is only that the role we play in the story we have learned does not belong to us. I was taught, as a child, that I was brave and beautiful, but also that I was fragile. The first story has helped me all my life, but believing that I was fragile has held me back. I was – and still am, if I am honest – scared to be open, scared to share and to shine all the wonderful things I have within me. I kept myself smaller than I needed to be because I believed that the world would break me. This story held me back for a long time. But then, slowly, gently, the Faery Queen has shown me that I can be as big as I am, I need not hurt myself by keeping myself small and hidden, I am not as fragile as I believed myself to be. I began to rewrite my story. I am sensitive, not fragile, and I am strong. Strong enough to face the world and stand my ground. I found some of my stories, the ones that served me I kept, the ones that did not, I rewrote. Since I began to rewrite this story I have felt stronger, I have healed an old injury and I have transformed my life into one of beauty and courage. There are still stories I wish to rewrite, but facing them, accepting that they are holding me back and that I have the power to change them, means accepting that I have chosen not to change them so far. This is painful, so I have compassion for myself; I take the rewriting gently and I understand the reasons I have not changed these stories yet. But I will. This is why I encourage you to uncover the stories you carry in your heart, the ones that help you and the ones that need to change for you to live the life you dream of. I know this transformative work is slow and not always easy, but it is so very worthwhile. You are both the hero and the author of the story of your life, you choose the stories you tell yourself and, if you choose them with love for yourself, you can write your story into something wonderful.

I offer you, then, love. Love for ourselves gives us the space to face our hidden parts safely and the compassion to rewrite our limitations in ways which benefit ourselves and those around us. Just as you made an oath to be honest, here is how you can use your magic mirror to relearn and remember how to love yourself when you forget.

Exercise 9. Facing Your Self With Love

Sit in a quiet space with your mirror and light a candle.

Breathe softly, imagine the golden light surrounding you, taking you into trance. Allow your heart to open as you breathe in beauty and breathe out tension.

Gaze into your own eyes in the mirror and relax.

What do you see?

Breathe.

Gaze into your own eyes and ask yourself, 'What is my heart? Who am I?'

Breathe.

Gaze into your own eyes and tell yourself: 'I Love you.'

Breathe and tell yourself, 'I Love You,' until you feel that it is true.

Breathe, rest, thank yourself and come back out of trance. Record your experiences and ground yourself.

Do something nice for yourself, as you would for a lover. Take yourself on dates, just you, where you can spend time getting to know yourself and showing yourself love. Be gentle with yourself, this is not an easy thing for most of us to do, but if you cannot love yourself, if you cannot treat yourself well, then how can you truly love anyone else? How can you help anyone else if you cannot help yourself? If we take care of ourselves then we are healthier, stronger and more joyful and so we are better able to help others. If we neglect ourselves we grow weak and ill and our inner light cannot shine into the world. Keep polishing your heart clean with love, keep caring for yourself with love and you will grow strong and healthy and joyful, able to share that joy with those around you.

There is no rush, treat yourself with love.

Show your fey side that you are a safe person to trust, so it can emerge. Know that, over time, by practising self-love you are offering your creative, intuitive, fey self a safe space to express itself within the world.

Love your Self.

Love those crazy, silly ideas that make you smile even if you don't feel like the world will understand – the Otherworld does, and so do the people who live with one foot in that world and both feet on the Earth!

Love your wild urges and sweet desires, your temper and your kindness, your passion and your sadness. Show your heart that there is room for all of you and give that fey spirit of yours the confidence to shine!

Chapter 6

Exploring Your Faery Heart

Walking on this path we have promised to be honest, we have begun to make space for our hearts in our lives, and we have learnt how to open our Faery Senses. Let us now put these things together.

Find somewhere comfortable to sit and play. Gather up your heart-box, your travel journal and your art supplies, so you can doodle, write, draw, paint, scribble and collage.

The next few pages contain prompts and suggestions for turning the Faery Senses on yourself and exploring your true self, your Faery Heart.

Writing and making art with your Faery Senses open allows you to see beyond what is normally obvious. The following three exercises can be done in any order or combined together. They work with the senses that are awakening within you. These are ways to explore what is important to you, what fills you with delight and what you might like to bring into your life to encourage enchantment to grow. They will help you discover what elements you would choose to have in your life-story by helping you to understand what is most truly you. Your Faery Heart, as that which you most truly are, is home to those things you love. Simply coming to recognize those things opens you to the possibility of making them real in your life and makes space for them in your life. Sometimes we hold things in our heart that are no longer good for us, like childhood toys kept in the wardrobe. They take up space and energy we could use for fulfilling our dreams. Sometimes we refuse to accept that we long for something specific and so we work hard to keep it out of our heart and mind, instead of recognizing and accepting that it is important to us. It could be because one of our stories tells us we cannot have it but, once we realize that we long for it and we accept it as belonging in our heart, our life, we can recognize that story and begin to rewrite it.

Open your Faery Senses in the way the Faery Queen told you. If she has not yet shown you how to open your own senses, repeat the Faery walk from earlier and ask her how to open your own Faery eyes and ears and then come back to your journal to play and explore your Faery Heart, the person you are before you forget your true nature.

The Heart-Box

You carry your Faery Heart with you every day, but you may not know much about it. We are taught to hide our deepest, untamed Selves and so we forget what we truly love. Using the heart-box as a reflection of your true Faery Heart you can explore what you hold dear, what you think you hold dear and what you wish to allow yourself to love.

As you come to learn about your heart, you should write down all your thoughts and feelings as over time they will show you patterns and you will come to understand the more hidden parts of yourself. This exploration will help you to know yourself and your true dreams, bringing you closer to making what you long for a reality.

Every true dream carries a touch of Faery and the more you become aware of your heart, the more you bring that magic into your life, healing yourself and the worlds around you.

Exercise 10. Finding Yourself Where You Are Right Now

Once you have your heart-box, take your box and your journal and find somewhere comfortable to sit. Breathe naturally, just slightly deeper than usual.

Imagine the golden light of beauty surrounding you as you breathe in beauty and breathe out tension.

Visualise your dream-temple in the land of your heart.

Imagine you are sat in your dream-temple with your heart-box. Does it look any different here? How does it feel?

Open your heart-box and peek inside. What is inside?

Breathe deeply while imagining yourself in your dream-temple with your heart-box. Allow your mind to focus on the box in your physical hands and place one hand over your heart.

Feel your heart beating, warming you. Listen to your heart and allow thoughts, ideas and inspirations to rise in your mind about your heart, your true heart. Here are some questions to help prompt you, take a few at a time and write down your responses:

- What makes you happy?
- What would you like to hold close?
- Who do you care about?
- What do you want to put in your heart-box, but are reluctant to?
- If you could do anything, what would you do?
- If you could be anything, what would you be?
- What do you love about yourself?
- Who are you?
- What parts of yourself would you prefer weren't true?
- What are your strengths?
- What are things you have difficulty with?
- What is the heart of your being?

There is no rush, just be open to your heart and you will know exactly what you need to when you are ready.

Feel how your heart-box feels to you as a representation of your Faery Heart. Is it missing things? Is it overflowing with love? Is it a little leaky? Are there some things you feel you would never put in there, but would like to just the same?

Record your experiences in your travel journal and get grounded.

When you feel ready to stop, close the boxes in both worlds and breathe deeply. Retrace your steps from your dream-temple and return to your body.

Record your experiences in your travel journal and get grounded.

Put your physical heart-box somewhere safe – perhaps on your altar – and know that this is a tool to help you explore where you are at each point in your journey.

Come back to this exercise as often as you like and see what arises. Repeat the questions at other times and see what changes. Keeping both worlds in your awareness will become easier with practice.

Exercise 11. Writing Your Faery Heart

Breathe deeply and imagine the golden light surrounding you. Breathe in beauty and breathe out tension and relax into the trance state, which is becoming familiar to you now.

Feel the mists between the worlds descend and feel your senses open. Know that you can see with Faery Senses, hear with Faery Senses, feel with Faery Senses. Sit with your journal and your heart-box and feel what belongs in your heart. Meditate or muse on these questions with your Faery Senses open so that you can see beyond the life you live now into the desires of your heart:

- What is in my heart?
- What fills my heart with love and joy and delight?
- What fills my heart with warmth, but I won't let myself hold?
- And what am I holding onto in my heart that I no longer need?

47

You might want to write or draw or doodle in your journal around these thoughts. You may suddenly realise you have the perfect thing to represent something you would like to hold in your heart and feel compelled to go get it and see how it feels to place it in your heart-box.

Allow insights to arise, take your time and record your experiences. Come back to this later and see how the answers have changed.

Exercise 12. Drawing Your Faery Heart

Breathe deeply and imagine the golden light surrounding you. Breathe in beauty and breathe out tension and relax into the trance state, which is becoming familiar to you now.

Feel the mists between the worlds descend and feel your senses open.

Draw a heart shape in your journal.

Breathing deeply and holding the sense of openness and wonder that comes from having your Faery Senses open, begin to fill the shape with the things that fill your heart with love.

Open to inspiration from the Faeries and breathe into the magic that surrounds you.

Allow yourself to collage, draw, write and doodle in the heart-shape, using the techniques that feel good and right to you to represent that which belongs in your Faery Heart, your heart-of-hearts.

If you wish you can muse on these questions to explore what is in your Faery Heart:

• What fills you with love?
• What would you like to hold in your heart, but are scared to?
• What do you know fills you with love, but you resist taking it in?

Surround the heart outline with things that support your heart, bringing your heart into the world. You can keep adding to this over time, allowing images to come to you in magazines or leaflets, or drawing them directly onto the page. Allowing words to arise, painting over images, cutting holes, drawing many hearts for all the parts of your life…anything that feels like it expresses what you feel would best fill your heart, and that surrounds you with a safe place to express your heart.

Be honest. Be as gentle with yourself as you need to be. Play!

When you feel you have done enough for today, gently put your art materials and journal away, breathe deeply and imagine the Faery mists fading away. The protective golden light that surrounded you gently fades too, still present if you wish it, but invisible so that it protects you and keeps you safe without getting in the way. Acknowledge the fact that you have been exploring your heart and notice how you feel. Make any notes you need to make and then get yourself grounded, coming back to your everyday life, knowing that you carry your Faery Heart within you and you are now blessed with a better understanding of what you wish your life to hold.

You may want to scan any images you make and print them out at card size so you can make them into a deck of cards, as I described earlier, to carry with you easily, or keep them visible around your home or workplace. You can make these images into wallpaper for your desktop, or posters for your room, or anything that helps you remember who you are. You may want instead to sit with the journal pages and condense them down directly onto a card, drawing or writing out the bits that most resonate into something that can remind you of the whole.

Experiment. Play. Enjoy.

Interlude:
A Short Thesis on Faery Anatomy

It is a well-documented fact that Faeries have wings. Unless they don't. But then they might have tails, or horns, or the legs of a dear, or a hollow head, or…let me start again.

Fae beings come in all shapes and sizes, often in a mixture of human and non-human parts, and very rarely plain. Being true to their nature, every fae being shines as extraordinary in some way.

What does this mean?

Since the fae are also often shapeshifters (being very rarely physical), what we see when they present themselves tells us something about what it means to be fey…

To be fey is to be winged with the power to fly as far as your dreams, and to display your true colours proudly.

To be fey is to be horned, crowned with horns, with the harmony of instinct and intellect to lead you truly on your path.

To be fey is to be extraordinary, to be so much yourself that you glow with it.

To be fey is to walk between the worlds of humanity and Mother Nature, true to your own wild heart.

To be fey is to be an edge-walker, a world-crosser, to be, in your heart, drawn to those liminal spaces in life and able to let your heart shine through your actions.

You do not need to be fey to be these things. There are other kinds of hearts, other ways, other lands…but those that are fey need to know, to accept and to express their particular heart-truth as fey.

To be fey is to be enchanted, to feel the edges of the worlds upon your skin and the core of magic in your heart. To be fey is to be an edge-walker with delight in and love for the world around you, and a deep sense that all is connected, all is alive, all is magic.

Exercise 13. Seeing Faeries
Faery beings are liminal beings, at the edges of civilisation. Coming into relationship with them brings us into relationship with our own natures, who we were before we were doing things because we should, before civilisation...and what we learn here about ourselves and about the world we can bring back into our daily lives. Beginning to see Faeries is a way to reintroduce wonder to our lives. Psychologically it gives our minds a framework for experiences where we recognise the value and magic of nature. Spiritually it opens us to the lessons of beings who have been here much longer than us. Practically it means that when we sense the fae, we are reminded of our own hearts, our own desires and deep longings, and our relationship to the world about us, and, ultimately, of the choices we are faced with: harmony or disconnection.

Seeing Faeries in our world is a slightly complex matter, partly because not everyone responds in a visual way to energies and spirits. For this reason, remember that when I say 'see', you may hear, or feel, or know that they are there. The way to know that it is more than your imagination is to practise being honest with yourself, and to watch for shivers up your spine, goosebumps despite the weather being warm, and other physical reactions.

Simply, to sense Faeries, go somewhere outside, preferably with lots of plants, somewhere that feels magical to you and is quiet.

Conjure up your golden egg of protective light.

Open your Faery Senses and sink into trance.

Breathe, and with each breath, imagine your heart opening to the fae, to the heart of the world that surrounds you.

Imagine your third eye, the point in the middle of your forehead, opening up.

Lay out an offering of cookies or something similar and

invite the Faeries near.

Now wait.

Don't strain to sense them, just relax and focus on keeping your heart open, soaking in the beauty around you, feeling the magic of the place, enjoy yourself.

I've found that reading aloud a beautiful poem about the fae often calls them, especially when it is read with heartfelt sincerity. Some folk find that singing to them calls them too.

Have patience and thank any fae that you meet.

Remember to close down afterwards, record your experiences and ground yourself. Take your time and return to this exercise often. This, as with most things, becomes easier with time. Keep a record of the kinds of things you sense. Not all fae are small and light and fast, many are slow and huge, or stately, or more like a swift wind than a butterfly.

Soon you'll be able to open your Faery Senses anywhere and sense the Faery beings that move through our world.

Chapter 7

Wild and Untamed Magic

On this path so far we have travelled into our hearts and we have begun to get to know ourselves and our fey hearts. This self-exploration is important before venturing into Faeryland itself as we need to be clear on who we are to be able to recognise the difference between our wishes and fantasies and true magic. With this understanding we have also made space in our lives to welcome the fey part of ourselves out to play, and have begun signalling to the Otherworlds that we are worth working with. Now, then, we turn towards the Otherworld beings that live in the world next door, the fae.

There are many different kinds of fae, and they can be classified using different models, for example:

Elemental fae include Gnomes (Earth), Sylphs (Air), Undines (Water) and Salamanders (Fire).

The Sidhe of Scotland are known to live in the Seelie court (beautiful and more-or-less moral) or the Unseelie court (uglier and less likely to help humans).

The fae as spirits of nature include Dryads (spirits of trees), Nyads (spirits of water) and Genus Locii (spirits of places).

Fae can be classified according to how they appear to humans; household fae, such as Brownies, helpful fae such as the Cornish Knockers, trouping fae, who look like lords and ladies or soldiers trouping across the land and so on or dangerous fae such as Kelpies (who drown the unwary) and Will O' the Wisps (who lead travellers astray).

All of these categories are interesting and can tell you a lot about our relationship to them, but the primary distinction you need to be able to make when approaching the fae is:

- Are they friendly and helpful, or not?

If they are not interested in working with you, are inclined to cause trouble or do not really understand the limitations of being mortal, then I would recommend leaving them be. Or in the latter case, approaching with caution and taking their suggestions with a dose of common sense! The classifications you will find are interesting, but so many fae transcend those limitations because they are, simply, less limited than we are.

Woodland Spirits and Urban Faeries

Anywhere there is life it is possible to find Faery magic, and thus Faeries. In woodland it is easy to find the spirits of the place and many Faery tales speak of going into the woods as the first step into an Otherworld, such as Pwyll in Y Mabinogi going hunting one day in the woods. Pwyll was rude to Arawn, the lord of the Welsh Otherworld, and so found himself making amends by living as lord of the Otherworld for a year and having to defeat Arawn's enemy for him, which Pwyll did very well at. The very next part of the story, however, has the Goddess and Faery Queen, Rhiannon, coming to find him and live with him as Queen in the city, so whilst we enter the woods to find the Otherworld, the Otherworld also lives alongside and within the cities.

Many of us live in urban areas. Even rural areas are often heavily managed and altered by human behaviour, so it can sometimes feel like there is little natural magic left. Just as we are part of nature, however, all life is part of nature and all things that are or have been alive have a spirit. Even in enclosed spaces, the air moves with the wings of sylphs as the rain-fae play outside. The spirits of nature in urban spaces also include the spirits of that most natural of expressions; music. One of the most Faery-filled evenings I have had was at a rock concert in

Nottingham's Rock City. The music filled the hall, the singer, Gary Numan, cast a glamour over the room with his stage presence, and the fae flocked around the rafters, riding currents of sound and the energy of the concert goers. The magic of music filled the space and the fae followed it. The fae are the spirits of nature and we are spirits of nature in physical bodies and so the magic we make most naturally is their magic.

We are never far from the big Mother Nature either, who manifests the blueprints woven into being by the song of the Faery Queen, even in the centre of a city you can reach her by stepping outside, gazing at the sky and breathing deeply. It is easier to feel her presence through green spaces, and in the growing things, and to meet the spirits of the land in less tamed places, but, again, remember that we are part of nature as much as the trees are, so Faery magic exists wherever life exists.

The main reason seeing Faeries is easier in more 'natural' settings is that those places are generally more peaceful and there is less interference, fewer distractions. If you are in search of urban fey, practise seeing Faeries in parks first and woodland if you can, and then find quiet spaces and times where you can watch for them in more built-up places. Using the Seeing Faeries exercise in a quiet garden or on a balcony at night can open windows onto the Faery realm. Watch for them at concerts and gatherings where people are happy and open and you will gradually find that the fae can be found as easily in a city as they can in a forest!

Exercise 14. Finding Faery Power Spots
Whilst at home, conjure up your golden egg of protective light. Slip a few silver coins into your pocket to leave as offerings.

Open your Faery Senses and sink into trance.

Breathe, and with each breath, imagine your heart opening to the fae, to the heart of the world that surrounds you.

Say a prayer to True Thomas, asking him, in your own words, to guide you to a place nearby where you can safely honour the Faeries and build a relationship with the local land-fae.

Feel your heart expanding and picture Thomas standing before you, ready to guide you. When it feels like he has arrived, stand slowly and follow him out of your home.

Visualise the golden protective egg becoming really strong as you step out through your door. Now let go of thinking about where would be a good place to go and let True Thomas guide your feet. Follow the gentle inspirations that feel as though they have just popped into your mind. Watch where you are going and choose the paths that are safe to walk. Those who feel light and positive are those that come from your guides.

When you find a space that feels good apply your common sense to the situation and check that it is a suitable place to sit and commune with the fae. State, aloud if possible, your intention to meet the local fae and ask if this is a place you are welcome. If you get a feeling of unease, as though you should move on, do so. If you feel comfortable and welcomed, stay. Introduce yourself to the spirits of the place and spend some time there, relaxing, breathing and listening for inspiration. Check back in with your golden egg periodically to ensure it is nice and strong.

In these kinds of spaces I like to journal as a method of listening. I'll doodle or write without a goal in mind and see what comes out on the page.

When you are ready, leave your offering with gratitude in a suitable place and return home via the route you came. Get grounded, make some notes and have something to eat.

This works as well in an urban space as it does in a rural setting. You might find yourself in a park, or a shopping centre. In the town I grew up in I used to find the fae perched on the stone lions in the centre of town, in the fountain in the local shopping centre or the peacefulness of the cemetery, as well as by the trees in my back garden and the lake on the other side of town. Wherever you are, remember to be aware of your environment and stay safe.

The spirits of places are the guardians of those places, in Heathenry they are known as Landwights and that term often accompanies discussions on how to be a good neighbour to those land-spirits that look after the landscape in which we make our home. Whether they are woodland fae, the spirits of rocks or mountains, or the spirits of lofty architecture, railway bridges or the hearthfire of a boiler, they are all spirits that manage the energetic side of the world we live within and are worth talking to. Make friends with them, leave them offerings and listen to their suggestions. As your relationship with them grows they will nudge you towards new places, useful tools (natural findings or charity shop bargains) and new learnings, as well as warning you of potentially dangerous situations just around the corner! In a city they can hide you and guide you as well as those in the wild can.

Offerings

Fae of all kinds appreciate gifts, given without thought of return, just as the host of a party will appreciate a thoughtful offering at the door or a friend loves to be remembered with a card through the post. When gifts are made to the spirits they are generally called 'offerings' and are made in the spirit of letting something go. Offerings are a way of saying 'Thank you' to the fae, of honouring them for their work in the living world and of showing them that we think of them and want to be friends, or at least good neighbours. Some things seem nice to us to leave as offerings, but can cause damage to the space we leave them in, such as tealight candles, which can spill wax, burn nearby plants or leave metal cases lying around once they've burnt out. Cheap tealights are also often made from petroleum, so burning them also releases chemicals into the air and uses up limited resources of oil. Certain foods are poisonous to other animals, such as chocolate (especially dark chocolate) and so if left out may be eaten by something and cause it harm. Good intentions go a long way with the spirit realm, but putting in a little extra thought to leave something that will give nutrients to the soil and won't cause harm to the beings whose home it is, is a more honourable thing to do. Glitter is a favourite of many Faery-loving humans because it reminds us of the joy and light they bring to our world, but glitter is often made of tiny particles of plastic or glass and it, too, can cause harm to animals. There is an alternative, however; biodegradable forms. Edible glitter is just as sparkly!

In an urban space, the parameters change again. Leaving a dried flower to rot away on an indoor fountain for the local Nyads is impractical as it will soon be tidied away by a staff member, and even edible glitter is unwelcome as it will make surfaces sticky when it gets damp. You can, however, throw a coin in a wishing well for the fae, and I will admit to feeding the previously mentioned stone lions sweets when I was small, as a kind of offering to the lion-spirits that watched over me when I walked through town. Coins are generally great offerings in urban spaces because they can then be given by the fae to people who need them, which is why finding a penny is good luck!

Exercise 15. Choosing Offerings

Have a look over the following lists and think about what suggestions might be suitable for where you live and which would not go down well. Go to your Faery power spots and ask the fae themselves what they would like. You can always negotiate if you get the response that they'd like something impractical, unsuitable or dangerous! What other ideas can you add to these lists?

Some traditional offerings:

- Milk and honey left in a dish
- Milk and honey poured on the ground
- Biodegradable ribbon tied to the branches of a tree
- A song or poem sung or read aloud
- A candle lit on your home altar
- Freshly baked biscuits

Urban offerings:

- Chalk kisses or hearts drawn on a wall or pavement
- A favourite drink poured over the roots of a tree or at a crossroads
- Sweets left in the mouth or hand of an appropriate outdoor statue
- Coins in a wishing well
- Money given freely to a busker or a beggar
- Extra tips to waiters or waitresses or donations in charity boxes
- Litter picking

Chapter 8

Faeryland

We open our eyes and the moonlight streams in.

The starlight glimmers at the edge of our vision and our heart, slowly revealing itself to our eager gaze, singing with the song of the stars.

We open our Faery Senses, just as the Faery Queen told us to, and the world becomes misty.

We step through the mist and the starlight is as bright as the day. The world around us sparkles and glows. Our hearts fill with delight and we sway, walk, dance through the world.

In the rustle of the leaves voices whisper to us.

In the patterns of shadow and light we see shapes flit.

In the spaces between the stars, faces smile down at us.

The Faery Sense is the ultimate in imagination. Imagination, the power that we have to build the world out of colours, shapes and sounds. Sounds and sights, all vibrations, all energy. Energy, flowing round us, sensed, built into a world.

Faeryland is the land at the edges of our normal consciousness, the realm of wonder and delight and creativity. It is, like our own world, both joyous and dangerous, the biggest risk being that we will lose our way, in or out, and remain stuck in one land or the other, unable to live in both.

At the edges of life as we know it, the heart of the world beats. The fae dance and hunt. And we can travel there, through the mists, into delight.

Just a quarter turn away, almost this world, but not quite, you reach out and almost touch it.

Lit by starlight; feasting, celebrating, fiercely alive, the fae beckon through the mists with their music. They reach out their hands as you reach out to them.

A soft brushing of fingertips, like kisses from a shy child or the momentary landing of a butterfly, makes the music louder, clearer. You find yourself dancing.

The vibrations of the Earth's heartbeat are a little faster than the physical world, the realm of Faery is a little higher than ours in the ladder of spirit which contains all – but only a little.

So close, all you need to do is breathe and let the music fill you, raise you up.

Their world pulled away from ours or, rather, we closed our eyes and ears to theirs.

In that time when we turned away from Faery, they never left. They worked even harder to wake us up, to show us the damage we were doing and help us to return to the playmates we once were. Their music plays through the worlds, showing us the way to return.

Entering into the starlight vision of Faery, the slanting of perspective that allows us to see the world in a new light, is the essence of opening to inspiration, to creativity. If Faery is the heart of life, then the Faery Senses are how we are to see life as alive as it can get.

To see a new face of things, as real as the face we see in everyday life, but more vital, allows us to understand ourselves and our world a little better. It is a way of seeing how everything is connected, all part of the same song, all part of the same nature. It is a way of freeing ourselves from artificial limits, from the constraints we impose on ourselves needlessly.

To visit Faeryland is to step into a world of possibility, where we can be ourselves, where we can meet parts of the world and come into communication with them, where we can learn about ourselves and the world and therefore, where we can come to know what is us, what we do to allow us to live comfortably with others, and what is unnecessary to our life, but we do because we feel we should.

We each have many roles in our lives: sibling, parent, grand-child, employer, boss, authority, student, teacher, golfer, artist, singer, bum, achiever and the many other roles we take on. Each of these roles we allow to define us. Each role we wear allows us to interact with others. Living with others is necessary, but we are more than just these roles. We are not just sibling, not just worker, not just student, not just anything. We are ourselves, taking on whichever roles we take on in life. We cannot be defined by these things alone. We may hold them in our hearts, we may be these things, but we are also ourselves.

Who are you?

Step into a world where you see each thing, each person, as it is in itself, and as it is in the great web of life, connected with all.

You are you.

And you are a part of all nature.

Step into a world where you can be you as a part of the world.

Using our powers of imagination we can change how we see the world, we can change our own minds. Find yourself somewhere comfortable and use your imagination to build the images below. Read through the journey a few times and memorise the basic steps, it need not be exactly as written here, allow yourself space to play. Visualise yourself doing these things and let the world build up around you. You can also record the steps to listen to it or have a friend read them to you, leaving pauses for events to unfold.

Now follows two journeys, one to meet a guide and one to travel with your guide to the wellspring of inspiration in Faeryland. They are best done first in the order presented on different days. They can then be repeated as often as you like, allowing for the experience to deepen each time. You will find that they are never quite the same twice in a row as the magic of Faery fills them and carries you to where you need to go...

As you may know from your reading of Faery tales there are a few rules to follow when travelling in Faeryland:

- Do not eat the Faery food (it will give them power over you, to keep you there if they choose)
- Be honest and respectful and do not stray from the path...until you know your way around!
- If anyone asks for help and you can give it, do
- If you are grateful, show it, but do not say 'Thank you' without meaning it

Exercise 16. Meeting your Faery Guide

On the path to Faeryland you will meet your Faery guide, the fae being who will guide you into Faeryland, who will teach you about Faery both within and without, for what better way to learn about a land than to be shown by a native? Settle down, breathe, and begin.

Open your Faery Senses and sink into trance.

Breathe deeply and allow the protective golden light to flow around you.

Feel a mist rise from the land and surround you.

Find yourself in your dream-temple, surrounded by the mists of Faery. Near your temple is a gateway, which opens onto a path through the mists. This path leads to Faeryland.

Visualise yourself moving through the mist onto the path to Faeryland. The path is not too wide and not too narrow. You can hear rivers roaring in the distance. The mist swirls around you, parting just enough that you can see the path you are to travel along. What lines the path? Which plants? Rocks? Trees?

Imagine yourself, feel yourself, moving through the mists and into Faeryland.

Up ahead you see a figure in the mists. This is your guide. Approach them with the willingness to work with them, to learn from each other, to perhaps become friends. Approach with respect, they've volunteered to be your guide in this land.

When you reach them, introduce yourself and ask what

you may call them.

Spend some time with them. They may just want to talk, they may offer you advice, or they may take you further along the path and show you some part of the land. If, at any point, you don't feel ready for something they suggest, thank them and say so.

Eventually it will be time for you to leave, say farewell to your guide, thank them and follow the path back to your dream-temple before returning to your body.

Exercise 17. Visiting Faeryland

Open your Faery Senses and sink into trance.

Feel a mist rise from the land and surround you.

Find yourself in your dream-temple, surrounded by the mists of Faery. Near your temple is a gateway, which opens onto a path through the mists. This path leads to Faeryland.

Visualise yourself moving through the mist onto the path to Faeryland. The path is not too wide, and not too narrow. You can hear rivers roaring in the distance. The mist swirls around you, parting just enough that you can see the path you are to travel along.

Imagine yourself, feel yourself, moving through the mists and into Faeryland.

Up ahead you see your guide waiting for you.

When you meet, you greet them and ask them to take you to the wellspring of inspiration and they lead you down a long path, the mists lift and you can see the land around you. You notice that everything is brighter here, the colours are somehow clearer, more vivid, more alive than back home. You follow your guide, ask them any questions you have and open to the answer.

What kind of land are you travelling through? What does the path look like? Are there forests or meadows, water or flame? What is the weather like? Are there other beings about?

Buildings? As you travel, notice your surroundings.

The path crosses a river that carries glints of gold in the light and a guardian stands at the crossing point. They offer you a challenge and they will only let you pass if you respond to their satisfaction. If they do not let you pass, return the way you came and try again another day.

If you do cross the bridge then soon, ahead of you, you see a gate across the path.

Behind the gate is the Wellspring of Inspiration.

Your guide gestures for you to enter; you open the gate and walk through.

The wellspring can take many forms, it is a golden light that runs like water and shines so brightly your eyes take a moment to adjust. When they do you notice a figure. This is the Keeper of the Wellspring. You may speak to them and ask, if you choose, how you are to find the inspiration of Faery in your life.

Perhaps they offer you words of wisdom. Perhaps they suggest that you bathe in the wellspring, or drink from it. Perhaps they give you a gift, or pose you a challenge. What happens here is between you and the Keeper.

When it is time to leave the Keeper will send you back, through the gate, to your guide.

And your guide leads you back along the path, across the river and home. Now it is time for you to leave, say farewell to your guide, thank them and follow the path back to your dream-temple, closing the gate behind you and returning to your body.

Breathe. Feel your body. Make notes and get grounded.

You now can travel to Faeryland whenever you wish. Spend some time getting to know your guide better, exploring the land around your dream-temple and yourself.

At any time you can travel to your dream-temple, just step

back into the mists onto the path and meet your guide. Ask them what you need to do, how to know your fey self better, how to find your way around Faeryland. They can give you suggestions on how to bring your Faery Heart more into your daily life, if that is what you want. Remember, though, to always temper what they suggest with common sense, Faeries don't always remember that we have work, or families who may not understand, or even that we are mortal and can't swim underwater for hours. Just use a little sense and you'll be fine, you can always tell them why you can't do what they suggest and ask if there is an alternative.

If you ever feel lost on the path you can take some time to talk to your guide, or, soon, to the Faery Queen herself, who knows Faeryland and the gates between our worlds as though they were parts of her own body. As when asking True Thomas for guidance you can sit somewhere quiet and comfortable, perhaps at your altar with a candle lit, breathe deeply and open the conversation with a prayer from your heart, or one such as these:

Prayer to My Faery Guide

Faery guide of my heart,
The path you see is clear.
I call to you in love and trust,
I ask you to be near.

And now, it is time to meet the Queen of the realm of magic, the Faery Queen who has called you here!

The Faery Queen

In the distance, you hear music, a soft, clear voice travelling through the mists that gather. It is the most beautiful song you've ever heard, filling your heart so full with wonder it feels like it will crack. You know this song is meant for you, it calls you, whispers to your heart of hearts of all the dreams you hold dearest. It is a love song, a song of celebration, an invitation. The singer knows what is held deepest in your heart because she is the ruler of that untamed realm, the Queen of all that is wild and joyful and magical on Earth. The singer is the Faery Queen, inviting you to meet her, where she can show you secret magic hidden in the land and your own soul...

If the fae are the spirits of the natural world, she is its soul. They are the energies that move through the land and speak to each plant, dance on each breeze, join together to hunt those whose time has come, bless the newborns, ease the passing of the dying and pinch those who need reminding to look where they're going! She, however, is Faeryland incarnate, the consciousness and director of all the magic of Faery, all the wild magic that runs through the world is hers to weave wonders with. She is the weaver of the magic of Faery, the centre of the cycles, the one who holds each fae spirit in her hands. She knows the big picture, watching and guiding how it unfolds.

The Faery Queen has been seen throughout mythology and literature in many guises. She is the archetype the Goddesses and characters embody. My Queen can be seen in Rhiannon of Y Mabinogi who came to our realm to rule with wisdom and compassion, or in the Nordic Freya who rules over magic, fertility and beauty, representing the growing of the green worlds and teaching trance-magic to the leader of the Gods. The Lady of the Lake, in her many guises, carries aspects of the Faery Queen, bringing magic to our world, as does Shakespeare's Titania, who reminds us through story of the magic in the wild places of the woods and the beauty and love to be found there. The Snow Queen shows us her harsher face when she brings the snows that freeze the land. This face of nature is hers too and without the frosts many plants would not know when to grow. Wherever an otherworldly Queen graces our world with magic, there the Faery Queen shows us a glimpse of her power. She is the force of nature with a consciousness, a power that is reflected throughout human history and who has much to teach we who have forgotten that the non-human world is as important as the human, and just as magical.

She is the one who has sent me to light this lantern for you, under the guidance of her Faery spirits. The Faery Queen knows that the natural world includes us and she has given us another chance to heal our relationship with our green, furred, finned and feathered siblings so that we can all survive the coming storms.

She knows that when our hearts are full of joy we help one another. She knows that when we follow our dreams we make miracles happen. She knows all this and she knows what is to come, and so she calls us, those that can listen, those that still dream, calls us to dance to the music of our hearts.

She stands for all the magic of the natural world, all the secrets of the fae, all the wishes of our hearts.

The Faery Queen, living in the wild heart of nature, can show us how our dreams, our wishes, our hearts fit in the world and how we can make them come true... She can also show us how to work with the green world to heal the rifts between the worlds. Let us heed her call and walk together, once more, through the mists to Faeryland to meet the Queen of Faeryland, the heart of the magic of the heart of the world!

Exercise 18. Meeting the Faery Queen

Open your Faery Senses and sink into trance.

Feel a mist rise from the land and surround you.

Find yourself in your dream-temple, surrounded by the mists of Faery. Near your temple is a gateway, which opens onto a path through the mists. This path leads to Faeryland.

Visualise yourself moving through the mist onto the path to Faeryland. The path is not too wide, and not too narrow. You can hear rivers roaring in the distance. The mist swirls around you, parting just enough that you can see the path you are to travel along.

Imagine yourself, feel yourself, moving through the mists

and into Faeryland.

Up ahead you see your guide waiting for you.

Greet them as before and ask them to take you to meet the Queen of Faery today.

As before, they lead you along a path through the mists, though on a different path this time. As you travel the mists clear and you see the land around you, take note of what you see, where you are.

Up ahead the path enters a thick forest of old, tall trees with splashes of light filtering through the leaves. The forest welcomes you as you enter with rustling leaves and creaking branches. Between the trees you might see birds, animals, insects or people; notice what is there as you pass deeper into the forest and the trees get bigger and closer. You can hear music, faintly but growing stronger with every step.

Suddenly the trees open out into a circle, a clearing in the forest lit by beautiful light.

Here are the musicians.

Here is the court of the Faery Queen, celebrating existence as they do every day.

Across the other side of the clearing you see a tall throne, upon which sits a woman more beautiful than any you have ever met before. She smiles at you across the court and beckons you to come to her.

Greet her with respect and wait until she invites you to speak, then you may ask whatever questions are burning in your heart and listen carefully for her answers. Talk with her a while. Spend some time with her and in her court.

Remember what wonders you see and hear here. Perhaps you are given gifts or offered words of wisdom to help you on your journey.

All too soon, it seems, it is time to return. Your guide indicates the path to return through the woods and you pay your respects to the Faery Queen and her court before leaving.

Your guide leads you back along the path, across the river and home. Now it is time for you to leave, say farewell to your guide, thank them and follow the path back to your dream-temple, closing the gate behind you and returning to your body.

Breathe. Feel your body. Make notes and get grounded.

You can now return to her court whenever you wish, or call to her for help when you need help understanding your path in the world, how you can bring your dreams to life, how you can reach the Faery magic, which is within you, and how you can help to heal the worlds. As before, you can speak from your heart, write your own prayer or use this simple rhyme to call to her:

Prayer to the Faery Queen
Green one, gold one, you who shine,
I bow to you and beg your time.
I heard your call and came your way,
I ask you which path to walk today.

Chapter 9

Daily Enchantments and the Spirit of Play

Faery magic is the magic of enchantment. It is the magic of connection and of the delight that comes from a playful wondering at the world. We are surrounded by beauty and joy, but our instinct is to focus on the negative (so we can avoid it, fix it, heal it, learn from it and save ourselves). Biology has made us this way for good reason, but in today's world we have access to so much information, we are surrounded every day by bad news and warnings and it often drowns out the magic present in every moment.

I believe my optimistic nature comes from the fact that my mother got rid of the television when I was ten years old. With no more news programmes to make me worry and panic and feel powerless, and no more advertising every 15 minutes to make me feel like I was lacking and worthless, I was free to build and create and know that I have value in myself and power over my life, to some degree at least. I now have access to all the information and news I might ever need via the internet, so I can be informed without being overwhelmed. I would recommend ditching the television to anyone and seeing how much happier you are...but back to Faeries! The reason I bring this up is because this is one of many ways in which we have become disenchanted as a culture, the subtle connections to magic and enchantment are hidden by the clamour of fear and want. The daily routine of work-eat-sleep leaves little energy for remembering those important relationships to the Otherworld beings that do not broadcast on the radio or have blogs (although I have received text messages from Goddesses, regularly use the radio as a divination tool and currently write the Goblin Circus blog according to the inspiration from the Goblins, so it isn't unheard of to find Faery mixing with technology!) So how do we keep that sense of enchantment and connection which we've built up during our work together?

Simple things done with a spirit of play work best, for example:

Use your altar and heart-box, keep a physical space for the fae and your feyness in your home as a reminder that the magic is there. Redecorate your altar when the seasons change, or at the old Celtic festivals of new life at Imbolc (around February 1st in the Northern Hemisphere), sensuality and sexuality at Beltane (May 1st), the harvest at Lammas (August 2nd) and endings, death and the ancestors at Samhain (October 31st).

Leave notes hidden where others can find them or written on the edges of bank notes and know that they will bring a smile to the faces of those who stumble across them. Leave notes to your future self in the same way to remind you of the magic you've found, hide them in books, the pockets of clothes, bags seldom used, the bottom of drawers and anywhere else you might stumble across them. Leave small gifts places, with notes saying, 'Free to good home', or, 'Please look after this Faery gift', in similar ways, as offerings to the re-enchantment of the world.

Wear body glitter or a particular scent as an expression of your fey nature. Each morning, after you've got ready for the day, take a moment at your altar and say a prayer to the Faery Queen to bless your day and guide you in enchantment. Put a dab of glitter or perfume behind your ears to remind you to listen to the messages of the fae, and over your heart to remind you to listen to the promptings of your fey heart. Faery festivals and events are great places to play and to express your fey nature. Find a way of dressing up that feels like expressing your fey self, it might be really subtle so no-one else would even notice, and dress up when you can. Take every opportunity to play and fill up your heart with enchantment and happy memories which you can draw on when times are harder.

If you feel overwhelmed, powerless or disenchanted, take some time to reconnect with your fey heart. Write in your journal, do some divination using the Heart Layout from this book or go for a Faery walk and remember who you are. You are fey, you are magical, you are beautiful and the holder of enchantment in a disenchanted world. By walking towards wonder and delight and allowing it to fill you and overflow into the world, you are performing an act of magic, an act of enchantment, in honour of the fae themselves. When you feel good, make a list of things that make you feel enchanted and connected so that when you have a grey day, and they do happen, you can look at your list and be inspired.

Imagine you have Faery wings that allow energy to flow in to your heart and back out to the world. Whenever you go outside, visualise your wings stretching out and soaking in the beauty of the world. In the book of Froud's *Faery Oracle*, Jessica Macbeth suggests doing this and including your Faery tail to ground you as well.

Grow plants and care for them. Sit with your plants or walk outside among trees. Breathe in life with every breath. Breathe out and know that your breath feeds the plants, just as their breath feeds you. Feel the connections between all things.

Put some music that fills you with joy on loud and dance round your room in the honour of the untamed spirit of your heart. Put the music on a portable music player and find somewhere outside to dance in honour of the Faeries.

Make a pendant, talisman, doll or other portable reminder of Faery. Open your Faery Senses and ask the Faery Queen to bless it for you. Carry it with you and touch it or look at it when you need to be reminded that everything is connected, and that there is joy in the world.

Always look to know your own heart and to act in accordance with it. Act with compassion; we are all connected, so hurting one, including yourself, hurts all, including yourself.

Listen to the messages of the Faery beings, especially when you are with green, growing nature, and ask for guidance in strengthening your connection to the Faery realm.

Listen to the song of your heart; what feels like the thing to do now that is most in alignment with your fey heart?

Each of these activities can be done as an offering, as an act of enchanting our own lives and a spell to re-enchant the world around us. Whenever you do anything that feels enchanting, ask the Faery Queen to bless that action as a spell to bring more enchantment into the world, and visualise the magic, wonder and delight you feel being magnified by her hand and spread into the world. Know that every time we increase the happiness and sense of wonder and connection to the world for ourselves and others we are combating the feeling of fear that keeps us isolated and fighting against each other, and it allows us to see the bigger picture a little clearer, including what we need to do as a community and a species in order to heal some of the damage that has been done to the land, our siblings of feather, fur and scale and to the climate on which we all depend. Every act of enchantment is an act of healing and honouring life and the magic of Faery, which underlies all of nature.

Going Further

Our journey together is drawing to a close, but the path stretches on before you. You have made space for Faery magic in your life and it will continue to draw nearer every day, bringing delight to fill your dreams. You have learnt new skills to open a world of enchantment and to begin the work of healing your life.

You have discovered parts of yourself long hidden, dreams

and wishes long denied and paths long forgotten.

You have learnt how to see the realms of Faery that lie nestled next to ours and to walk into Faeryland itself to bathe in inspiration and speak to the Queen of the realms of magic.

Every step you take upon this path heals the rifts between the worlds and in learning to know your true heart you bring the dreams it holds fully into this world. The best way to continue working with the fae and Faery magic is to meet up with your guide, using the visualisation from before if that helps and to ask them for guidance and suggestions, but remember they are real beings and always approach them with respect.

Perhaps you could ask them to introduce you to the Faery King.

Perhaps they will show you methods of Faery healing.

Perhaps they will help you create things that reflect some of Faeryland into our mundane world.

What happens from here on is between you and the fae. I can only suggest that you follow enchantment and use your common sense. We cannot physically fly, poisonous plants are poisonous even if recommended by spirits and sometimes our own issues get in the way of hearing what they suggest clearly. If it sounds like your own fears talking, then it might be worth thinking about it and perhaps beginning work on those issues with a professional before continuing.

If you ever feel lost, confused, or unsure of how to proceed, revisit the exercises with the heart-box from earlier to clarify how you are feeling now. What in you has shifted since last time you checked in with yourself? Where should you be heading now? You might find or make yourself a system of divination, say a deck of tarot or oracle cards, a set of runes, a pendulum, or whatever suits you best. This can help you to think, and give you a nudge in the right direction. You can also pray to True Thomas, your Faery guide or the Faery Queen herself for guidance.

Epilogue: My Green Heart

Changing our Perceptions or Dying of Consumption

In the world today we have mass extinctions, a huge division between rich and poor, children starving to death every day and war on every continent. We are addicted to a source of power that is finite and causes yet more problems from pollution to defor-estation. Even in many of the rich countries of Europe, America, the land of the free, and all the other so-called Western countries of plenitude, even there so many people are miserable, poor, stressed, struggling, depressed, desperate for meaning...self-help books, escapist entertainment and consumer products marketed as providing meaning abound, leaving the consumer even less satisfied in the long run, just placated for a moment.

I've written this book because I can see a need for a revolution, a revolution towards the heart. Our world is disenchanted and I am an Enchantress, dedicated to re-enchanting the world. My work is to return wonder to the world, a pixie kiss and goblin dance at a time.

This book is my invitation to you to join me in this work.

There are people all round the Earth who are reaching for a world that lies closer to their heart and, for me, following the call of the fae opens a door to that world. Knowing our own hearts allows us to follow them, listening to the heart of the world means we can see the path through the world, we can hear the tune that we can choose to come into harmony with. Then, and only then, we can allow that music to spill over into our lives and to bless those around us.

This journey to Faery, for me, reveals the need for us as humans to recognise our place as a part of nature. The things we make, therefore, are natural too. This does not, however, give us free rein to do as we like, but means that we must look at our lives as such, as interconnected and as in relationship to the rest of the natural world.

If our actions affect others and their actions affect us then maybe our actions should take this into account? And if we are a part of nature, connected to it, dependent upon it for survival, health and happiness, then perhaps we should take this into account too?

Once we foster a relationship with the rest of nature as if it were sentient, sacred and valuable, as if, in short, it were inhabited by the fae, then we can build a relationship whereby we take advantage of our modern-day, Western-culture technology and privilege, but also feel connected and fulfilled, also have a sense of place, a sense of meaning, a sense of helping and being helped. If we treat nature with respect, then we will not chew up all of our resources through arrogance. And if we see the fae in the world, then we can foster some of that wonder so many of us feel has been missing since childhood or before.

There is no reason to give up the advances we have made technologically, but there is every reason to harness them in a way that allows us to live within our means on this planet, and in harmony with the natural world, remembering that harmony involves both give and take. We need to eat, but if we strip all the food for ourselves, everyone suffers. Now, even more than ever before, we can see the effects of climate disruption. The weather is extreme, species are going extinct every day, our world is dying, but there is still hope. As long as we act out of fear and hide from what is happening, nothing will change and the world as we know it will end. But we have a choice, now, to open to love, to know ourselves and fiercely follow that sense of enchantment wherein we bring ourselves back to our place in the web of nature, and let go of our desire to control it all to allay our fears.

And so here I am, writing for my part in a revolution of the heart.

Open, listen, follow your heart and remember that all of nature has a heart too.

When I consciously stepped onto the path of the Faery Heart and began actively working with the fae again, in a way I hadn't since I was young, I felt my heart open.

In this opening I found certain old beliefs came to light, convictions I held, but had chosen to ignore. The more I opened, the more I found those convictions called to me...and the fae voices echoed them, reflecting them back like a mirror.

We are animals, part of nature. And all is divine. Nature, as all, is divine, and so sacred...and to live as though all is sacred means to treat the world as sacred. To live in harmony with the natural world of which I am a part I need to take steps in my life to live more sustainably, I have looked and looked and it is clear to me that we humans are out of balance with the rest of the world and that this can lead to no good.

And alongside this, the Faery voices that whisper at the edges of my hearing, the clear messages from my guides, and the song rising in my opening heart, all pointed to the same thing, for me. This is what I heard, for myself:

You are part of nature, look after yourself and the world around you.
  Without the Earth, where would you live?
  How would you feel if there were no more trees to walk in? If all the rivers are full of rubbish? If you cannot swim in the sea?
  How can you eat the animals when you don't need to?
  How can you justify causing so much damage when you are one of us, another creature of this Earth? It'll hurt you too, you know.

I found myself reminded of my 'green' convictions, my beliefs – backed up by scientific evidence – that we are all connected, the whole world and all her creatures. I am just another animal and, by extension, every other animal has as much right to live and live well as I do. My life, when I stepped onto this path, did not match these convictions. I started to walk to the beat of my own ethics.

I had begun to walk the Faery path, my path of the Heart, and yet, I had far to go.

And so, as the blue full moon graced the skies and soft white snow covered the world making a fresh page, I made a choice, a choice I saw years before, but was too scared to follow through...

I chose ways in which I can live my life more in harmony with the natural world, of which I am a part, more in harmony with the fae, as fey myself. And the fae supported me; they help me with every step I take towards harmony between the worlds.

I chose, as I stepped onto this path, to live as fey with a green heart. To honour nature, to create beauty and to seek and share delight through my life. I made an offering of my life in the hopes that I can help to re-enchant a world that has fallen into disenchantment. I chose the path of the Enchantress, for which opening my fey heart was the first step.

I write this to the sound of Leonard Cohen singing his anthem, of the imperfect offering, cracked to let the light in. I can only do what I can and I am not expecting perfection, but I have an offering. An offering for myself, and for the fae, and for the world. My heart is cracked, and the light shines through. I can see my way, my path, my choices... What choices do you make? What does your heart tell you? What convictions will you choose to commit to in order to walk your fey-hearted path?

What is your Faery Heart? Your Faery magic?

May you walk each day, step by step, into the light of your True Heart, your core. May you know who you are, may you do what you can each day, as imperfect and beautiful as that may be, to act on what your heart says. And may you remember that you are not alone. All around the world, others are walking the same path, by the light of their Faery Hearts.

Walking with you,
~Halo Quin xx
In the heart of Wales where the Faery Queen Rhiannon rules,
Beltane, 2015

Your Faery Magic

Resources and References

Halo Quin, *The FeyHearted Oracle* – A 40-card deck produced by myself, based on my experiences and philosophy of the Faery world, and printed in very short runs on demand. Find it on my website at www.aworldenchanted.com/faery

Brian Froud and J Macbeth, *Faery Oracle* – An oracle deck based on Froud's Faery paintings with a useful book. Very evocative.

R. J. Stewart, *The Living World of Faery* – Full of exercises, suggestions, inspirations and stories of the fae. As he has a strong connection with the Faeries and a deep knowledge of their folklore and history, Stewart's other books on Faery are also well worth investing in.

T. Thorn Coyle, *Evolutionary Witchcraft* – Not strictly Faery, although primarily based on Thorn's branch of Feri, which is very fey. This is a good book for practical, ecstatic magical techniques.

Orion Foxwood, *Faery Teachings* – A student of R. J. Stewart, Foxwood writes about the Faery Seership Tradition.

Rob Hopkins, *Transition Handbook* – This is about the Transition Movement, based on permaculture principles. It presents information on the way our culture currently operates, how that relates to peak oil and climate change, and suggests ways of transitioning away from oil dependency. I would recommend it as an introduction to these topics, and for information on how to transform your life gently in ways which bring you more into alignment with the rest of nature.

Dianne Purkiss, *Fairies and Fairy Stories: A History* – Tracking the history of human relationships through Faery tales, disclosing the nature of Faeries as shared through stories woven through the years. It is an illuminating book with an academic leaning, and not at all dry.

Robert Kirk, *The Secret Commonwealth of Elves, Fauns and Fairies* – One of the earliest written accounts of Faeryland, originally dated 1961 though first published in 1815, *The Secret Commonwealth* was a risky thing to write. Collected by a church minister, it documents the experiences his flock in Scotland had of the fae, Faeryland's connection to the realm of the dead, and other fae related curiosities.

Sorita D'Este and various authors, *The Faerie Queens* – An anthology published through Avalonia Press on the many guises of the Faery Queen throughout myth, legend and literature. (In which I have an essay on Rhiannon, Faery Queen of Wales.)

Sheena Frost, *Soulcollage*[TM] – a guidebook for creating your own Oracle deck using collage and ritual.

Music Mentioned
Queen, 'A Kind of Magic', *A Kind of Magic*, (EMI, 1986)
Leonard Cohen, 'Anthem', *The Future* (Columbia, 1992)

MOON

BOOKS

Moon Books invites you to begin or deepen your encounter with Paganism, in all its rich, creative, flourishing forms.